The Best
Stage Scenes
# of 2005

Smith and Kraus Books for Actors
MONOLOGUE AUDITION SERIES
The Best Men's / Women's Stage Monologues of 2004
The Best Men's / Women's Stage Monologues of 2003
The Best Men's / Women's Stage Monologues of 2002
The Best Men's / Women's Stage Monologues of 2001
The Best Men's / Women's Stage Monologues of 2000
The Best Men's / Women's Stage Monologues of 1999
The Best Men's / Women's Stage Monologues of 1998
The Best Men's / Women's Stage Monologues of 1997
The Best Men's / Women's Stage Monologues of 1996
The Best Men's / Women's Stage Monologues of 1995
One Hundred Men's / Women's Stage Monologues from the 1980s
2 Minutes and Under: Character Monologues for Actors Volumes I and II
Monologues from Contemporary Literature: Volume I
Monologues from Classic Plays 468 BC to 1960 AD
The Ultimate Audition Series Volume I: 222 Monologues, 2 Minutes & Under
The Ultimate Audition Series Volume II: 222 Monologues, 2 Minutes &
    Under from Literature
The Ultimate Audition Series Volume II: 222 Monologues, 2 Minutes &
    Under from the Movies
The Ultimate Audition Series Volume II: 222 Comedy Monologues,
    2 Minutes & Under

SCENE STUDY SERIES
The Best Stage Scenes of 2004
The Best Stage Scenes of 2003
The Best Stage Scenes of 2002
The Best Stage Scenes of 2001
The Best Stage Scenes of 2000
The Best Stage Scenes of 1999
The Best Stage Scenes of 1998
The Best Stage Scenes of 1997
The Best Stage Scenes of 1996
The Best Stage Scenes of 1995
The Best Stage Scenes for Men from the 1980s
The Best Stage Scenes for Women from the 1980s
The Ultimate Scene Study Series Volume I: 101 Short Scenes for Groups
The Ultimate Scene Study Series Volume II: 102 Short Scenes for Two Actors
The Ultimate Scene Study Series Volume III: 103 Short Scenes for Three Actors
The Ultimate Scene Study Series Volume IV: 104 Short Scenes for Four Actors
Scenes from Classic Plays 468 BC to 1970 AD

If you require prepublication information about upcoming Smith and Kraus books,
you may receive our semiannual catalogue, free of charge, by sending your name
and address to Smith and Kraus Catalogue, PO Box 127, Lyme, NH 03768. Call us
at (888) 282-2881; fax: (603) 643-1831 or visit www.smithandkraus.com.

Published by Smith and Kraus, Inc.
177 Lyme Road, Hanover, NH 03755
www.SmithKraus.com

© 2006 by Smith and Kraus, Inc.
All rights reserved
Manufactured in the United States of America

First Edition: January 2006
10 9 8 7 6 5 4 3 2 1

Cover illustration *The Stagehand* by Lisa Goldfinger
Cover and text design by Julia Hill Gignoux

The Scene Study Series 1067-3253
ISBN 1-57525-430-1

NOTE: These scenes are intended to be used for audition and class study; permission is not required to use the material for those purposes. However, if there is a paid performance of any of the scenes included in this book, please refer to the Rights and Permissions pages 210–214 to locate the source that can grant permission for public performance.

The Best
Stage Scenes
of 2005

edited by D. L. Lepidus

SCENE STUDY SERIES

A SMITH AND KRAUS BOOK

Contents

Scenes for One Man and One Woman

Scenes for Two Men

Scenes for Two Women

Foreword

The scenes in this book have been drawn from the best plays published or produced during the 2004–2005 theatrical season. All are from published, readily available plays (see the Rights and Permissions section at the back of this book for publisher information). Many of the scenes herein are by playwrights of considerable reputation, such as Howard Korder, Nilo Cruz, Stephen Adly Guirgis, and Wendy MacLeod. Others are by future stars such as Julian Sheppard, Eric Coble, Tristine Skyler, John C. Picardi, and Mark Schultz.

Most are scenes with characters under forty. I made a conscientious effort this year to find some terrific scenes for teen actors, such as those from *Common Ground, Schoolgirl Figure,* and *Everything Will Be Different.*

In short, this is the best darn scene book I could put together. I know you will find in it the perfect piece for your audition or class use; but if you want more options, check out Smith and Kraus' other fine scene collections.

Many thanks to the agents, authors, and publishers who have allowed me to include these wonderful scenes in this book.

D. L. Lepidus

Scenes for
One Man and
One Woman

ANNA IN THE TROPICS
Nilo Cruz

Dramatic
Conchita, twenties to thirties; Juan Julian, thirties to forties

> *This Pulitzer Prize–winning drama takes place in a cigar factory.*
> *Juan Julian is a "lector," which means he reads to the workers while*
> *they roll cigars. Conchita works in the factory. She is unhappily mar-*
> *ried. In this scene, a romance blooms between the lovelorn woman*
> *and the lector.*

CONCHITA: How did *you* become a lector?

JUAN JULIAN: I discovered books one summer. My father owed a lot of
money to a creditor and we had to close ourselves up in our house
and hide for a while. For my family, keeping up appearances was important. We had to pretend that we had gone away on a trip. We
told neighbors that my mother was ill and she had to recuperate
somewhere else. We stayed in that closed-up house for more than
two months, while my father worked abroad. I remember it was hot
and all the windows were kept closed. The heat was unbearable. The
maid was the only one who went out to buy groceries. And while
being closed up in our own home my mother read books to the family. And that's when I became a listener and I learned to appreciate
stories and the sound of words. *(Smiles.)* Have you ever been to New
England?

CONCHITA: No.

JUAN JULIAN: I always wanted to go there. I wonder what New Englan-
ders are like. Here I have met workers from other parts of the world,
but I haven't met anybody from up North.

CONCHITA: Cheche is from up North.

JUAN JULIAN: Cheche is from a world of his own.

CONCHITA: I knew a fellow from New London. He was modest and reserved. So shy was this boy, that when he expressed any sort of

feeling, he would excuse himself. *(Laughs.)* One day I gave him a braid that I'd cut from my hair and told him to *bury* it under a tree. I explained to him that back in the island most women cut their hair once a year on the second of February, when plants and trees are pruned, for the feast of Saint Candelaria. I told him how women offer their hair to the earth and the trees, for all the greenery and fruits to come. And I gave him *my* little braid in a box and told him to choose a tree in the park.

And the boy looked at me with a strange face and said that he would feel embarrassed digging a hole in the middle of the park, in front of everybody. And that's when I took my braid back from him, took a shovel, dug a hole and put him to shame. From then on he never talked to me again. So he's the only person from New England that I've met. *(Palomo enters. He watches from a distance.)*

JUAN JULIAN: *(Laughs.)* And do you still cut your hair every second of February?

CONCHITA: Yes. My father always does me the honor of burying it.

JUAN JULIAN: Your father! And why not your husband? It should be an honor for any man . . . If I were your husband I would find an old, wise, banyan tree and I would bury your hair by its roots, and I'm sure it would accept the offering like rainwater.

CONCHITA: Well, I'm cutting my hair short like Clara Bow and that will be the end of the ritual.

JUAN JULIAN: I would offer to find a strong-looking tree. But the ritual won't count if it's not done on February second.

CONCHITA: I believe everything counts if you have faith.

JUAN JULIAN: So are you telling me that I should pick a strong-looking tree?

CONCHITA: Yes, if you wish.

JUAN JULIAN: And why me?

CONCHITA: Because you offer to. And you are the reader of the love stories, and anybody who dedicates his life to reading books believes in rescuing things from oblivion.

JUAN JULIAN: So is there a story in your hair?

CONCHITA: There will be, the day I cut it, and that story will come to an end.

JUAN JULIAN: And how does one read the story of your hair?

CONCHITA: The same way one reads a face or a book.

JUAN JULIAN: Then we shouldn't bury your hair under a tree. We should place it inside a manuscript. The same way Victorian women used to press flowers or a lock of hair between the pages of a book.

CONCHITA: Then I would leave it to you to choose the book.

JUAN JULIAN: How about this one?

CONCHITA: My hair will be in good company with *Anna Karenina*.

JUAN JULIAN: Then close your eyes and choose a page. *(Conchita closes her eyes. She opens the book and chooses a page. Juan Julian reads:)* "At first Anna sincerely thought that she was annoyed because he insisted on pursuing her; but very soon after her return from Moscow, when she went to an evening party where she expected to see him, but which he did not attend, she came to the realization by the sadness that overwhelmed her, that she was deceiving herself."

CONCHITA: Then here, cut my hair. *(Conchita hands him the scissors. She loosens her hair and turns her back to him. He combs her hair with his fingers. He kisses her shoulder. She then turns around to return his kiss.)*

BRIGHT IDEAS
Eric Coble

Comic
Joshua and Genevra: twenties to thirties

> *Joshua and Genevra are parents of a small child. They are obsessed*
> *with getting their child into the top pre-school "Bright Ideas," which*
> *at present is full. Here, they plot to bump off another parent.*

JOSHUA: *(Kissing her.)* You're a genius. You are such a genius, you . . . are
a genius genius genius —

GENEVRA: What'd I do?

JOSHUA: You got our son into "Bright Ideas"!

GENEVRA: How?

JOSHUA: Inviting Denise over. Oh, God, you're good.

GENEVRA: I'm insane. We can't have her over for dinner — the place is a
pigsty, I'm going out of town

JOSHUA: I'll clean it. I'll take care of everything —

GENEVRA: And how is that going to get Mac into "Bright Ideas"?

JOSHUA: . . . Oh come on! You invited her here! You know!

GENEVRA: . . . No. It was totally on impulse. I should never act on impulse. We joined that CD club on impulse, I bought that striped
swimsuit on impulse — when are we gonna learn?

JOSHUA: Listen, listen, listen. You said yourself she's set for life —

GENEVRA: God. Her parents helped pay for the pre-school aquatics room
and she just happens to get in? What kind of system is that?

JOSHUA: Exactly. And she just got a new Land Rover, right?

GENEVRA: Right. Which reminds me, did you do both car payments this
month?

JOSHUA: Not yet. I have to wait for my next check to cover that and the
cable and the six-hundred we owe the tutor for Mac's entrance exams.

GENEVRA: If the Adams account falls apart, it takes my bonus with it.

JOSHUA: It's not gonna fall apart.

GENEVRA: Nobody is repossessing our cars. I don't care *if* the MasterCard people show up with a SWAT team, they are not taking our cars —

JOSHUA: We're not losing our cars. You're gonna kick ass on the Adams account, my raise comes up in three months — we can survive 'til then —

GENEVRA: Why does it have to be this hard? I can't even breathe.

JOSHUA: Do you think Denise has any trouble breathing?

GENEVRA: No.

JOSHUA: So we point this out to her. We're salesmen, Gen. We have a nice meal with her, nice wine, and we sell her on the idea which is the truth — that she and her son do not need "Bright Ideas" pre-school to get a foothold in this world. We do.

GENEVRA: That's your plan? *(Josh nods.)* Sweetheart, I love you but that is the most asinine thing I've heard all day.

JOSHUA: We're really good salesmen, Genevra.

GENEVRA: No one is that good. Forget the wine — we could give her crystal meth and airplane glue and she won't let go "Bright Ideas."

JOSHUA: I'm trying to visualize something positive here, Genevra. You're not helping —

GENEVRA: Visualize something plausible.

JOSHUA: Like what?

GENEVRA: Like I don't know. Like we buy her out.

JOSHUA: We're gonna have trouble pulling together that first tuition payment, much less —

GENEVRA: I'm trying to visualize something positive here, Joshua.

JOSHUA: OK. Money. We can get money. We can join a class-action lawsuit against the slide manufacturers —

GENEVRA: We need the money Wednesday, not when he's forty —

JOSHUA: Money Wednesday . . . Money Wednesday . . .

GENEVRA: Maybe we can sell some of your parents, stuff off e-Bay —

JOSHUA: Right, OK, see, there are ways — money will come. *(Running in place.)* Burning lava, Gen, burning lava — run with me — chant — burning lava — we have the power to make this happen —

GENEVRA: If we get her drunk —

JOSHUA: We could get her drunk —

GENEVRA: She'd fight it in court when she's sober. I don't even know if she drinks.

JOSHUA: What about extortion? We get some dirt on her, threaten to go public with it unless she drops out?

GENEVRA: What dirt?

JOSHUA: I don't know — dirt! You work with her — what are her secrets?

GENEVRA: I hardly know her!

JOSHUA: Well, get to know her!

GENEVRA: That's what the dinner is for!

JOSHUA: Burning lava . . . burning lava . . .

GENEVRA: Please stop running. It's like thinking in a fitness club.

JOSHUA: I think I can sell her, Gen. I really think we can open her heart to do what's right —

GENEVRA: I've been on management retreats with her. Her heart does not open.

JOSHUA: If she meets Mac — sees his little face —

GENEVRA: She's gonna laugh in his little face and ours and everyone else's that she's ever stepped on to get to the top and she's never gonna change!

JOSHUA: OK, fine! Let's just kill her and get it over with! How's that, huh? You like that plan? *(He keeps running . . . She pauses . . . they stare at each other . . . he stops running . . . a long, long pause . . . then . . .)*

GENEVRA: Um. What you just said . . . I'm not sure that we should —

JOSHUA: It was a joke, Genevra.

GENEVRA: Of course.

JOSHUA: I'm just throwing out ideas, I'm not recommending a course of action —

GENEVRA: Thinking outside the box, that's good. *(Beat.)*

JOSHUA: . . . But as long as we're thinking . . . I think we might as well think through this one too. That way if any parts of the idea have any viability whatsoever —

GENEVRA: Which they won't.

JOSHUA: Of course not. *(Pause.)* She's divorced, right?

GENEVRA: Right.

JOSHUA: Husband lives in . . . ?

GENEVRA: Chicago. New wife.

JOSHUA: So her son, should something happen to his mother, does have a place to go.

GENEVRA: Yes.

JOSHUA: A fine, loving, wealthy family where he'll be well taken care of.

GENEVRA: But which would mean he'd have to drop out of "Bright Ideas." *(Pause.)* I can't believe we're talking about this —

JOSHUA: It's just ideas, Genevra. Ideas never hurt anybody.

GENEVRA: *(Pouring a glass of Remy Martin.)* I need a drink.

JOSHUA: Her son is, what, three?

GENEVRA: Yeah.

JOSHUA: How much do you remember from when you were three?

GENEVRA: Not much.

JOSHUA: Like nothing. Your brain puts all that stuff in a box marked "Do not open until death or intense therapy."

GENEVRA: Right.

JOSHUA: So the chances of this kid getting permanently scarred by something like this are like . . . zero.

GENEVRA: She's a human being, Joshua. Denise is a human being.

JOSHUA: Is she more human than us? Does her son deserve happiness any more than ours?

GENEVRA: No, but he doesn't deserve to have his mother whacked by two homicidal parents either!

JOSHUA: And we don't deserve to have our son's future ripped out from under us because we didn't buy the aquatics room! We're not talking about "fair," Genevra! Is it "fair" that Denise got to go to . . . where did she go to school?

GENEVRA: I don't remember.

JOSHUA: Well, it was someplace great, I'll tell you that. She did not have a garbage man and a housecleaner for parents

GENEVRA: Don't drag them into this!

JOSHUA: Well then, speaking for myself, she didn't come out of a hardware family that considered donuts after bowling the epitome of luxury. She didn't have rats scurrying around her bedroom at night — you have nightmares about ducky wading pools? Well, try having them about rats chewing your toes off! Denise had no mountains to climb to get here, Genevra. She had no hills! She had no bumps of earth! Everywhere she ever needed to go, anything she needed to do, she was driven in a nice car with the top down! And now her three-year-old son has the keys to the same damn car and he's stepping on the accelerator and we can't even climb into the damn trunk! Where's the fairness, Genevra? Who's looking out for us? Who's looking out for Mac? *(Pause.)*

GENEVRA: We're talking about murder, Joshua.

JOSHUA: Yeah. Yeah, we are. And we're talking about our son's future. About giving him a life we never got to have. Everything we're sweating blood to hang onto can come easy to him. We're this close, Gen. This close. Mac can't get out of the roots and the wading pool by himself. He needs us. Do you want to save him or don't you?

GENEVRA: What if we end up in jail — what kind of life does he get then?

JOSHUA: I'll make sure we don't get caught.

GENEVRA: How?

JOSHUA: I don't know. It has to look like an accident.

GENEVRA: But nothing to hurt her son.

JOSHUA: Of course not.

GENEVRA: . . . There's a website . . . where they list bad foods — mushrooms, berries, hallucinogenic seeds — things you never put on a kid's pizza . . . There might be something we could put in the food . . .

JOSHUA: But we're all gonna eat the food.

GENEVRA: Of course we are, but we don't eat what she — I don't know why I'm even talking about this! This is impossible, it's your sick fantasy! She's just going to come over to dinner and we're gonna have a nice time and . . . and . . . and . . . *(She's out of ideas.)*

JOSHUA: *(Quietly.)* And on Monday, her kid will start his life and ours will end up in some podunk school eating staples and he'll have to fight just to stay alive, just like his parents did. Bravo.

(Handing her a book.) Go read to your son. God knows somebody's gotta teach him.

BUICKS
Julian Sheppard

Dramatic
Bill (early thirties); Naranja (early twenties)

> *Bill is married, with two children, and owns a Fresno car dealer-
> ship. He is miserable in his life. The only person who seems to re-
> spect him is Naranja, his secretary, a Mexican immigrant who wants
> Bill to sponsor her for her green card. Bill's wife has left him, tak-
> ing the kids. Desperate to find them, he hits the road, bringing along
> Naranja for emotional support.*

BILL: Wow. Albuquerque. That the longest you ever been in a car?

NARANJA: No.

BILL: Crazy adventuro we're havin', huh? Crazy on the road. Best thing
I've done in ages! God, I feel — I feel alive. Discovering America!
This how you pictured America, Naranja?

NARANJA: Yes.

BILL: You know this exact — this exact motel room you could find in
every state across the union. Uh-huh. Every truck stop pit stop town
across the country, this exact room, walls, wallpaper, desk, bed, TV,
bathroom. All the same. Kinda comforting, yeah? Kinda comforting. Kinda bizarre too. Wonder if there's two people, just like us, in
some motel room in what, Pennsylvania? Or Georgia? Two people,
just like us . . . God, I am all wound up. Need to chill out, y'know,
get my bearings . . . plan o' attack. Know what I mean? Shit, shower,
shave, go over and see what the story is!

NARANJA: Should you call your wife and tell her you stop and you are
OK? *(Bill turns off the TV.)*

BILL: My wife knows I'm fine.

NARANJA: I just do not want her worrying.

BILL: My wife knows I'm fine. *(Beat.)* So you make it to Fresno, now you're getting your green card — pretty exciting! Now what? I mean I guess you can stop being scared of getting caught and deported all the time.

NARANJA: . . . Yes.

BILL: Does anything really *happen?*

NARANJA: I become more like real person —

BILL: Yeah, what does *that* mean?

NARANJA: I get green card, maybe my life . . . more like your life?

BILL: You don't want my life.

NARANJA: I take your life.

BILL: Well now Naranja, I may have lots of authority, but my life's not the barrel of laughs it looks like!

NARANJA: It seem OK to me.

BILL: Sure it does. So how you gonna get my great life?

NARANJA: I do not know . . . maybe I could sell cars, like you?

BILL: Well, sure, there's a great idea.

NARANJA: I be a good salesman for you.

BILL: Oh yeah? Well all right. Sell me a car.

NARANJA: What? Right now?

BILL: Yes, right now. It's so easy, go for it. Knock me out.

NARANJA: I — OK — you are not tired Mr. Abeline?

BILL: I'm completely exhausted. *(Quick beat.)*

NARANJA: Do you . . . do you like this model?

BILL: Yeah, sure, whatever.

NARANJA: No whatever, sir. I tell you secret, you not tell anybody. The Park Avenue is easily my favorite model of all the cars on the lot. Do you know why? I bet you know what I am thinking . . .

BILL: No . . .

NARANJA: It is the strongest-looking of all the cars on the lot. It has a style. People, they often say, Buicks, not a stylish car. But this model — I think it really has a *flair.* And you would look exceptional driving it. You would look . . . strong.

BILL: Hm. You think?

NARANJA: Absolutely. And it is not just that it has this style. I feel it is the car which is right for you. Let me tell you why. Power and comfort. This is what the Park Avenue has. Power. Comfort. I see that you are a man who need the extra horsepower you can only get with the special supercharged V-6 engine that come with the Park Avenue. You would like to have that little extra kick, yes, who would not?

BILL: Yeah, a little power'd be good.

NARANJA: But you also need the extra comfort — the extra *luxury* of the Park Avenue. Ten-way power front seats — you, as you should — would have absolute control. This feature only comes in our Park Avenue. Also available in our Ultra package, only in the Park Avenue, are heated front seats with lumbar adjustment. You and your lovely wife — what is your wife's name?

BILL: Millicent.

NARANJA: You and Millicent are taking a long drive on a beautiful chilly winter night. It is romantic. You feel in control of the road with your four-speed automatic transmission, your antilock four-wheel disc brakes, your supercharged 3.8 liter V-6 engine. You and your wife are comfortable. But you are . . . a little cold. And your back is a little stiff. You are a tall man. You need space for breathing. In the Park Avenue, you have the highest combination of front leg room and head room of any our spacious Buick models. You would ride in great comfort, with great power at your fingertips. The Ultra package, which I am sure you would be interested in, goes for merely thirty-eight thousand one hundred dollars. I think one test drive will suffice to show you that the Buick Park Avenue is the best car for you. Shalt we take spin, or wait for your lovely wife, Millicent?

BILL: Wow. I don't think I give you enough work to do.

NARANJA: No. You do not.

BILL: And you were so demure about trying it out. When you let go, you sure let go.

NARANJA: You think is good sales pitch? I have never said it out loud to a person before, and you are my boss, you are the expert. Was it good? I like the heated seats. Are they stupid? What do you think?

BILL: Well, you should never just make up random lies to hook the client.

NARANJA: What lie?

BILL: Park Avenue your favorite model?

NARANJA: I have heard all you lie to customers.

BILL: But not randomly. Only when the lie plays into something they've said. That way it's a lie they want to hear.

NARANJA: OK.

BILL: And are you sure you want to intimate to the client that you'd sleep with him?

NARANJA: Excuse me, Mr. Abeline!

BILL: What? The "strongest-looking car"? You'd look "strong"? What do you think, you know, a client would think?

NARANJA: I do not know what you are talking about.

BILL: Yeah, that whole bit, I don't know. Don't hint that you'd sleep with him, let him do all that work.

NARANJA: OK, good, yes. So you think my sales pitch, it is good start though, yes?

BILL: Sure. Yeah, sure. What's your Thing?

NARANJA: My what? My Thing?

BILL: Your Thing. The Thing that's the reason people should buy this car from *you.*

NARANJA: You mean instead of Jared or Tim?

BILL: Yeah, but more — what can *you* tell them? That only *you* know, only you can convey that will make them say "I'm going to buy this car." That's what sells cars. Your Thing.

NARANJA: What do you convey? What's your Thing?!

BILL: I can't tell you.

NARANJA: I would not steal it.

BILL: That's not — it's not something you can just *say.* It's . . . in you. But it's not just this vague — it's what you're selling. It's who you're selling. What you want them to have in them after they buy the car, when they're driving the car six months, a year, two years later, even if they don't know it. *Especially* because they won't know it. And you have this Thing there, at your disposal, if it feels right. It doesn't always. But sometimes you're sitting there with the client, with this person who wants a *reason,* and this is how you can give it to them. How you can make yourself be understood. A thought, at the tip of your tongue. A belief. And it just comes out of you. Effortless. Like . . . pure motion.

NARANJA: And you can do this?

BILL: I — sure, I don't know. Forget it. I mean, not everybody — my Dad never had a Thing and he could sell cars to a blind man in a snow-storm.

NARANJA: I must find a Thing.

BILL: Yeah, yeah sure.

NARANJA: So you are giving me job?!

BILL: Thought I was giving you my whole life.

NARANJA: Do not make funny of me! You give me advice. Why give me advice if you not giving me job! Do not make funny of me!

BILL: I — I wasn't — hey there Naranja, whoa.

NARANJA: I am doing you favor! You need new business, same people always come in.

BILL: There are new people all the time.

NARANJA: Look like same people. You need a little color. Expand business. Sell some Mexican people cars.

BILL: Have you ever even been in sales?

NARANJA: I have been in sales.

BILL: Where? In Mexico?

NARANJA: Yes! I work at big tourist hotel. At front desk.

BILL: You checked people in.

NARANJA: Yes —

BILL: That's not sales.

NARANJA: It is sales. People come from all over world, I must make things OK, make them still think is good hotel even if we mess things up. I work in Manzanillo, it is major tourist destination, there are many other hotels, they go somewhere else. This is sales!

BILL: That isn't sales, it's customer service.

NARANJA: There is this one time this Swedish man come to the hotel. He have terrible trip. His luggage lost, he get wallet stolen at airport, he get sick from airplane food — he is not happy. He come to hotel and his room is not available, somebody mess up. He must get smaller room. I never see someone so angry and so sad. But I take him up to room, I show him it is nice room. I make him feel OK, about the room. He like everything in it. This — I sell him.

BILL: All right, that's good customer service.

NARANJA: Uchh, you not understand.

BILL: Look, I'll think about it.

NARANJA: Fine. You think about it. But this car will not sit here without you forever. *(Bill laughs.)*

BILL: . . . Nice.

NARANJA: Maybe is a good thing we go on this trip together. Very entrepreneurial.

BILL: Naranja. I'm . . . I'm exhausted. Need to regroup.

NARANJA: What about the funeral?

BILL: It's not 'til later . . . I'll just — I'm — I'm sorry about the bed. This was the only room they had.

NARANJA: I am not tired now. You sleep.

BILL: Are you sure? *(Naranja shrugs. Beat. Bill closes his eyes. Beat.)* What the hell is Manzanillo anyway? Thought you were from Zacaton?

NARANJA: Zacaton, Zacaton is nowhere. Manzanillo has job, I go to Manzanillo. I work at one of the best hotels in all of Manzanillo. It is very glamorous, it is right at the beach. It is really so beautiful right there on the beach. The rest of town, it is just Mexico, but the ocean and the beach . . . And the job, I am lucky to have it, everybody keep telling me. It is not easy job, but I am good at it. At selling to all these people who come from all over, to my little corner of the world. At making things be OK for them. Even when I do not want to. But this — this is why I think maybe I can sell cars, like you! *(Naranja realizes Bill is asleep.)* OK. *(Beat.)* Do you understand all this, Mr. Abeline? *(As Bill:)* I sure do, Naranja. But that doesn't sound so bad! Try being me! *(As herself:)* OK, Mr. Abeline. *(As Bill:)* I'm kidding! Ha ha ha! *(As herself:)* You know, this is the first time since I come to America I have been in a bed with a man. *(As Bill:)* Really?! You don't have a boyfriend you have sex with at that bar you drink tequila at? *(As herself:)* No no no. No boyfriend. No family. Nobody at all. *(As Bill:)* That is so sad. You are so sad. *(As herself:)* Thank you, Mr. Abeline. *(As Bill:)* Buenos noches, Naranja. Sleep well. *(As herself:)* Good night, Mr. Abeline. You sleep well too. *(Beat. Blackout.)*

COMMON GROUND
Brendon Votipka

Dramatic
Kylie and Blake, late teens.

> *Kylie and Blake are nearing the end of their time in high school.
> Here, they discuss their lives while sitting in a coffee shop.*

KYLIE: How well do you think you know me?

BLAKE: What kind of a question is that?

KYLIE: I was just wondering.

BLAKE: I think I know you pretty well!

KYLIE: OK. OK.

BLAKE: We've been best friends since we were three, I know you better
than anyone I bet.

KYLIE: We have been friends forever.

BLAKE: Right. So I know you. If anyone knows you, I know you.

KYLIE: OK.

BLAKE: Think about all the time we've spent together. Remember play-
dough.

KYLIE: Play-dough buddies to the end.

BLAKE: Remember when we dressed up your little brother like an elephant,

KYLIE: And we made him stand on the street corner and sing that song,

BLAKE: And we told him he couldn't have a Popsicle until he got at least
three dollars from people walking down the street.

KYLIE: What about when we kept your sister in a box!

BLAKE: Oh my gosh, I forgot about that! That was a great box.

KYLIE: She actually liked it!

BLAKE: What about Mrs. Gregory's class.

KYLIE: She was the worst. And Mr. Turner's class.

BLAKE: That was so much fun.

KYLIE: Remember the first day of seventh grade.

BLAKE: And the clothes we wore!

KYLIE: Remember the first day of high school,

BLAKE: We swore to stay best friends forever.

KYLIE: Yeah. We did.

BLAKE: We're still best friends, right?

KYLIE: We have so much of a past.

BLAKE: Right. We're still best friends.

KYLIE: How well do you think know me?

BLAKE: We've been best friends forever.

KYLIE: I'm not saying you haven't known me in the past. But in the two years since we made our pact. Do you think you still know me as well as you did when we were kids? Because I'm not sure I still know everything about you, like I used to.

BLAKE: I still think I know everything about you, whether or not you know me.

KYLIE: What's my favorite class this year? Who was the last person I had a crush on? What movie did I see most recently? Is my favorite color the same as it was in junior high?

BLAKE: Red.

KYLIE: Blue. *(Kylie leaves and Blake is left alone. Long pause.)*

CRASHING THE GATE
Frederick Stroppel

Seriocomic
Sarah and Dooley: twenties to thirties

> *Sarah and Dooley are terrorists, waiting for the word to commit a bombing. During this scene, they receive word that the plans have changed.*

SARAH: *(She answers phone.)* Falcon here.

DOOLEY: *(Scornful.)* Falcon . . .

SARAH: *(Into phone.)* Yes . . . The moon is in the seventh house. Is the heather on the hill? . . . *(Sarah looks at Dooley and nods her head, "It's them" Dooley gives a sarcastic thumbs-up.)* Yes, we're ready for further instructions. Please advise . . . What? There's a partridge in the pear tree? *(Confused.)* What does that mean? . . . Really? Oh wow. No shit.

DOOLEY: What? What?

SARAH: *(Into phone.)* Yeah, I see . . . So what do we do? . . . Uh huh . . . Uh huh . . .

DOOLEY: What?

SARAH: Well — you want to talk to him yourself? . . . *(Dooley reaches for the phone, but Sarah doesn't offer it.)* Oh. OK. No, I understand. We have to adjust . . . Well, it is what it is . . . Yeah. OK. Roger, over and out.

(Hangs up.)

DOOLEY: Are you gonna tell me what, or what?

SARAH: Change in plans.

DOOLEY: What?

SARAH: The drop is off.

DOOLEY: The drop is off?

SARAH: Something must have leaked. All of a sudden they have guards set up, surveillance cameras . . . It's a whole new deal.

DOOLEY: Shit! See? You see? We should have done it last week! I told them!

But no, we have to wait! Fucking pussies! All this James Bond bullshit with phone messages and code names, and now the whole mission is fucked!

SARAH: It's not fucked. The mission is still on.

DOOLEY: Yeah, right, we're just gonna improvise something now, after all that meticulous planning? Burns my ass! Wasting our time sitting around in this dump — no cupcakes . . . ! Ahh . . . ! *(With resignation.)* You know what? Whatever. They're running the show. Whatever they say. New plan? Why not? Let's hear the new plan. I'm sure it's good. Jasper came up with it, so it must be fucking brilliant. Let's hear the brilliant new plan.

SARAH: *(Deep breath.)* OK, well . . . It appears we're gonna have to crash the gate.

DOOLEY: *(Scoffs.)* Yeah, right.

SARAH: *(Serious.)* No, right.

DOOLEY: We're gonna crash the gate?

SARAH: Well, you. You're gonna.

DOOLEY: I'm gonna?

SARAH: You're the driver.

DOOLEY: So I'm gonna crash the gate, and then what?

SARAH: And then set off the bomb.

DOOLEY: Set it off with what?

SARAH: With a button — I don't know. You're the Munitions Expert.

DOOLEY: So I set off the bomb, and then what?

SARAH: And then the bomb goes off. I think that's the logical progression.

(Beat.)

DOOLEY: Let's go over this, so I can get it clear in my mind: I'm in the truck, and the bomb's in the truck, and I crash the gate, and I set off the bomb . . . There's a crucial step missing here. Mainly, what the fuck happens to *me?*

(Long beat.)

SARAH: See, the mission has *changed.*

DOOLEY: *(Understands.)* Now it's a suicide mission.

SARAH: Uh huh.

DOOLEY: And I'm the suicide.

SARAH: Uh huh.

DOOLEY: So I'm dead.

SARAH: Basically.

(Beat.)

DOOLEY: Gotta say, that's a little harsh.

SARAH: It's a regrettable development, to be sure.

DOOLEY: I really didn't sign up for that!

SARAH: You pledged yourself to the cause, didn't you?

DOOLEY: The cause won't do me any good if I'm dead.

SARAH: Sometimes we have to make sacrifices for the sake of our guiding principles.

DOOLEY: My biggest guiding principle is staying alive, and I can tell you right now, I'm willing to sacrifice *anything* to preserve that.

SARAH: Unfortunately that's not an option. The fight for liberty, as history teaches us, is a stark and bloody one. We're trying to reclaim our birthright as a free people here, and if we have to pay the ultimate price to secure that freedom, then so be it.

DOOLEY: So why don't you do it?

SARAH: I can't drive a stick.

DOOLEY: I'll teach you. It's not that fucking hard.

SARAH: Look, they want *you* to do it. Those are the orders.

DOOLEY: They can go fuck themselves. I'm not getting myself blown up into a million pieces for their amusement, no way.

SARAH: *(Brightly.)* Maybe you won't get blown up. I mean, with all those guards, you might actually be shot dead before you even reach the gate.

DOOLEY: Oh, I didn't realize there was a silver lining.

SARAH: It's definitely a tough break, but what are you gonna do?

DOOLEY: What am *I* gonna do? I'm gonna pack my things and get the fuck out of here.

SARAH: What do you mean?

DOOLEY: I mean I'm booking. I'm out.

SARAH: You can't be out.

DOOLEY: *(Packing his things.)* Sorry, but this isn't my thing. I don't want to kill a lot of innocent people.

SARAH: You didn't mind killing them before.

DOOLEY: That was different. That was a surgical strike against a symbol of oppression — there was nothing personal about it. This way — driving right up to a crowd of people just standing there drinking their coffee — that's vicious, man. It's like playing God, and I'm not into that scene.

SARAH: I think you're just afraid to die.

DOOLEY: Bin-go! I'm not one of those Al Qaeda wackos, thinks he's gonna spend eternity in paradise screwing a bunch of virgins. I want my reward now, on earth, thank you.

SARAH: Well, I gotta say. I'm a little disappointed in your attitude, Dooley.

DOOLEY: *(As he gathers the cards on the floor.)* And your approval means so much to me right now.

SARAH: No, I thought you were the real thing. I thought You had real balls.

DOOLEY: Oh, I have real balls. They hang on either side of my dick, and that's where I plan to keep them. I like that arrangement.

SARAH: This is such a great opportunity for you. You're gonna become a legend, do you realize that? This is your dream. They'll write folk-songs about you, put you on *A&E Biography* . . . Just like James Dean.

DOOLEY: I don't really give a fuck about James Dean. I never did.

SARAH: And on a personal note, I'll always be proud to say that I worked with you.

DOOLEY: *(Intrigued.)* Yeah? *(Then he dismisses it.)* Nice try. You and your fucking feminine wiles. This was probably your idea in the first place.

SARAH: You heard me on the phone. I didn't say a word.

DOOLEY: Because it was all in code. "The heather on the hill" and all that shit. You and Jasper, working your little conspiracies, trying to kill me.

SARAH: Why would we do that?

DOOLEY: Because I'm a threat to the organization. I speak my mind, I challenge authority, and that scares you guys. You want everyone to be a fucking lemming, following orders, and you're afraid some of those lemmings will start following me — the man with the common touch, the true leader.

SARAH: Who's gonna follow you? You don't even have the guts to drive a itty-bitty truck through a tiny little gate.

DOOLEY: I'm an American, and Americans don't commit suicide. That's part of our national character. We fight, we rebel, and we win! Our founding fathers — not one of them look the pipe. Not even Benedict Arnold. So call Lover-boy and tell him to get another stooge, somebody from a foreign country, where life is cheap. I'm outta here.

SARAH: Dooley, think hard about this: If you make the wrong move, it could haunt you the rest of your life.

DOOLEY: And if I make the right move, the rest of my life will be about two hours long. No thanks. Bring on the ghosts.

(Dooley starts out the door but Sarah blocks him.)

SARAH: We have to complete this mission.

DOOLEY: You complete it. *(Mimics a stick shift.)* Reverse, neutral, drive, second, third. It's like an "H." Piece of cake. *(He hands her the truck keys.)*

SARAH: You can't just walk out like this, Dooley. You have an obligation.

DOOLEY: I didn't sign any contract. This was a labor of love for me, and frankly the love is gone.

SARAH: Then you'd better try to fake it. Or else.

DOOLEY: Or else what? You're gonna revoke my membership?

SARAH:Or else you won't live to tell the tale.

DOOLEY: *(Mockingly.)* I won't live to tell the tale? Are you kidding with that shit . . .?

(Dooley moves toward the door again, but Sarah pulls out a gun.)

DOOLEY: *(A shocked laugh.)* What the fuck . . . ?

SARAH: OK? So make up your mind.

DOOLEY: You're not gonna shoot me. *(As Dooley moves toward her she jabs the gun at him and he prudently retreats.)* OK, OK, don't be a fucking hero. *(Beat.)* Can we talk about this?

SARAH: Nothing to talk about. I have my orders.

DOOLEY: You have orders to get rid of me? That fucking Jasper . . . !

SARAH: You can't back out of a mission. That's not an option.

DOOLEY: So my choices are, kill myself or be killed. This is your idea of freedom? *(Shakes his head.)* I knew I shouldn't have got involved with you people. Should have gone out on my own, been a lone vigilante, a sniper or something. Fucking organizations are all the same. I joined the Boy Scouts when I was a kid, and that was bullshit, too. So political. *(Beat.)* That's a nice gun. Where'd you get it?

SARAH: Peabody's Gun and Ammo. Floor model.

DOOLEY: Can I see it? *(Sarah just stares at him.)* There's something fucked up in this country when somebody can own a gun, but she can't drive a stick shift.

SARAH: What's it gonna be, Dooley?

(Beat.)

DOOLEY: Well, I'm not gonna let some girl shoot me. *(He puts his things down.)* Might as well go out in a blaze of glory. Start building the legend.

SARAH: *(Lowers the gun.)* All right then. They change shifts at 15:30 — that's 3:30 — so there'll be lots of activity and confusion. More people, more potential collateral damage, bigger media exposure — hopefully they'll preempt *Oprah*. It takes about twenty minutes to make the trip, so we have about half-an-hour to prepare. You'd better rig up the truck.

DOOLEY: That'll take two seconds. Maybe I'll go out and get myself a last meal. Cupcakes, hopefully. *(As Sarah follows him to the door:)* You don't have to come with me.

SARAH: Yes I do.

DOOLEY: You don't trust me? Jesus. You'd think, being a martyr, I'd get a little more respect. What are you gonna do, hold that gun on me right up to the moment we explode?

SARAH: I guess so.

DOOLEY: *(Realizes she's serious.)* What, are you crazy?

SARAH: You have a job, I have a job.

DOOLEY: Don't be fucking stupid. Stay out of it.

SARAH: I can't, now.

DOOLEY: What's the sense in both of us getting killed? Look, Sarah — I promise, I'll go through with the mission. I'll blow myself up. I'm starting to look forward to it. But you have to live. Who's gonna tell my story to the world? Who's gonna do my *60 Minutes* interview?

SARAH: We're a team. We go down together.

(Beat.)

DOOLEY: *(Sighs with resignation.)* Fucking fanatics. Nothing but trouble.

SARAH: *(With growing enthusiasm.)* This is a great day, Dooley. We're going to wake up the world. This country is dry and withered, and ready to burn. All we have to do is light the match. The moment is here, the moment is now. *(Holding her gun high.)* Thirty minutes to Armageddon! All aboard!

DOOLEY: So you want to screw around before we go? You gotta be pretty fucking distracted by now. *(Sarah glares at him.)* You know, Sarah, you're probably a very good revolutionary, but you're kinda cold on the personal level.

SARAH: I'm focused. I'm committed. That's why I joined the organization. I'm not sure why you joined.

DOOLEY: Frankly I was hoping to meet women.

SARAH: And you met me.

DOOLEY: Yeah. Ha. *(Shrugs.)* Well — nothing left to do but wait, I guess.

SARAH: I guess.

(Dooley picks up the deck of cards. He sits and starts flipping the cards into the wastebasket. Sarah pulls up a chair beside him, and watches. Dooley cuts the deck, and hands half to Sarah. They both sit back and flip cards into the wastebasket.)

ELOISE & RAY
Stephanie Fleischmann

Dramatic
Ray, twenty-eight; Eloise, sixteen

> *Ray is walking Eloise home after a first date, which has not been
> sanctioned by her father. Ray is the former best friend of Eloise's older
> brother, Jed, who disappeared when Eloise was nine years old, at
> the time her mother died. Jed has recently returned to Ovid, Colorado, after seven years in jail.*

ELOISE: Stop! You can leave me here.

RAY: Here? You sure?

ELOISE: Oh, I'm sure.

RAY: I'm coming with you.

ELOISE: No you're not. *(Taking off.)* You can't.

RAY: *(Grabbing her arm.)* Your brother would skin me alive if he got wind
    I didn't accompany you to your door.

ELOISE: *(Walking ahead.)* Well he ain't gonna hear.
    *(Ray catches up to Eloise. They walk in place, backs to audience, faces
    in profile, the Super-8 film road rolling away before them.)*

RAY: He's got big ears. Runs in the family.

ELOISE: Thanks a lot.

RAY: Except that yours are like a fawn's.

ELOISE: I ain't no deer:

RAY: And your eyes —

ELOISE: What else I got of his?

RAY: You got this.
    (He hands her a walnut.)

ELOISE: A walnut?

RAY: It was his. You can have it if you want.

ELOISE: For good luck?

RAY: If you can call it that.

ELOISE: You kept it all these years?

RAY: In my pocket. *(He looks at her.)* Look at you. His eyebrows, his chin. His legs, maybe. Do you know, he was my legs. *(Their hands brush each other as they walk. Ray grabs on to hers.)*

ELOISE: You got a pair of your own right there. *(She pulls away.)*

RAY: No. You don't understand. He kept me moving when it hurt like hell to walk because he knew that walking was better than staying still.

ELOISE: Everybody knows that.

RAY: No, he was my legs.

ELOISE: Your legs?

RAY: Until the day he ran and I got stuck.

ELOISE: You're not stuck.

RAY: No. Look at me. Here, with you.

ELOISE: Ray.

RAY: What?

ELOISE: The day he ran — ?

RAY: *(Impatient.)* What!?

ELOISE: You remember the day he ran — ?

RAY: No. Can't say that I do. It was a long time ago.

ELOISE: OK. If you say so. *(Beat.)* Why did it hurt?

RAY: What?

ELOISE: To walk.

RAY: It just did. My joints. Ever since I was yay high. Ridin' the horses helped. And then there was your mother.

FLOISE: My mother?

RAY: Used to make a boy feel like he could talk. A teenage boy full up to here with trouble.

ELOISE: Trouble.

RAY: That pain in my joints and this knife forever turning in my stomach. Got so bad sometimes it made me want to do things.

ELOISE: I know what you mean.

RAY: Made me want to twist my neck like a corkscrew until I'd popped right out of my skin. But your mother —

ELOISE: My mother.

RAY: Pull up a chair and talk to me, she'd say. On her good days.

ELOISE: On her good days.

RAY: And I would. She wasn't afraid to listen. And when I was done, she'd tell me stories.

ELOISE: Stories?

RAY: Family stories, mostly.

ELOISE: I didn't know we had any.

RAY: Not yours. Stories from books.

ELOISE: Right.

RAY: She loved to read.

ELOISE: I know.

RAY: She liked Shakespeare. I remember that.

ELOISE: Shakespeare?

RAY: She read that stuff all the time.

ELOISE: I don't wanna hear about her. Talk about Jed. Tell me what he was like.

RAY: You're his sister. You tell me.

ELOISE: My brother Jed was the only person I could ever talk to besides Rosanna and my mother on her good days.

RAY: You could talk to me.

ELOISE: I don't hardly know you. My brother Jed called me his girl Eloise. My mother always said it was Jed who taught me how to walk. Walk and talk.

RAY: Nobody taught you. You did it for yourself.

ELOISE: I did it for him. My brother Jed taught me three chords on the guitar and now they are strung inside me like DNA. They are the music inside my head.

RAY: Will you play it for me? That music?

ELOISE: I dunno. Maybe. It's Jed's.

RAY: Will you — Can I kiss you?

ELOISE: I dunno. Maybe.

(They kiss their first kiss.)

RAY: My girl, Eloise.

HATE MAIL
Kira Obolensky and Bill Corbett

Comic
Dahlia and Preston, thirties

> *Dahlia is a successful photographer. Preston is someone she hasn't seen*
> *for a long time. He works in a hospital.*

PRESTON: A Leica camera. Why do you ask? Are you a connoisseur? I've
been told I have a discerning eye.
(Silence.)
Anti-Leibovitz? Are you still there?

DAHLIA: It's me.

PRESTON: You?

DAHLIA: Yes. Me.

PRESTON: YOU! . . . Oh my god, I need a shower!

DAHLIA: Jesus, I feel sick! Have you been trailing me?

PRESTON: No! I didn't know it was you, I swear!

DAHLIA: I don't know how you've managed to insinuate yourself into my
life again, after two years

PRESTON: I didn't! I'm not!

DAHLIA: I have to go. My husband needs me.

PRESTON: Oh. Is he — ?

DAHLIA: . . . Immensely successful well-balanced handsome athletic sen-
suous witty nurturing reads a lot my life is rich filled with activity
and spiritual fulfillment? Yes, he is.

PRESTON: And yet you cruise the net at night in search of cyber-sex.

DAHLIA: No, it's just . . . the technology fascinates me.

PRESTON: Sure it does.

DAHLIA: Well . . . I have my own goddamn house in Seattle now. And
have you seen my pictures in *Rolling Stone? Interview? Elle? Der
Spiegel?*

PRESTON: Yes.

DAHLIA: Jealous?

PRESTON: Yes.

DAHLIA: Bitter?

PRESTON: Yes.

DAHLIA: Good.

PRESTON: But —

DAHLIA: What?

PRESTON: But — at the same time — happy for you. A *little* bit.

DAHLIA: How does that work?

PRESTON: I don't know. But even in that sea of bitterness, there's always been a tiny lifeboat of pride in your accomplishments. Of me wishing you well. It's gotten tossed violently at times, been smashed down into a small piece of driftwood, but still it bobs up and down —

DAHLIA: Stop it, Preston. But thank you. What are you doing?

PRESTON: Drinking generic beer and eating Kraft singles from the pack.

DAHLIA: I mean with your life.

PRESTON: I'm a doctor. Well, I work in a hospital. Well, actually I'm an orderly. Trainee.

DAHLIA: Glad to see you're still thinking small.

PRESTON: Glad to see you're still the Queen of Compassion.

DAHLIA: Ha! You finally have to work for a living, like the rest of us peasants, huh?

PRESTON: Thanks to you. All right, I'm not crazy about minimum wage, but — I mean this! — I love my job. Really! These sick old people in my hospital —

DAHLIA: What, they're "sweet," or something?

PRESTON: Not at all! They're fucking *impossible:* perpetually crabby, always bitching and moaning as I empty their bedpans and give them sponge baths. But somehow I . . . miss them on my day off. It seems I like them.

DAHLIA: Hmmm. You've changed.

PRESTON: Maybe.

DAHLIA: I think I've changed too. Remember how neurotic I used to be?

PRESTON: I seem to recall, yes.

DAHLIA: How I felt like this fake, this creepy stealer of souls: Diane Arbus, only not as mentally healthy? Well, I don't question myself anymore. Not at all.

PRESTON: You shouldn't. You're extraordinarily talented . . . you always were.

DAHLIA: *(Suddenly ten years old.) Really?*

PRESTON: Really.

DAHLIA: And you always were . . . kind. Sometimes.

PRESTON: Sometimes I always was kind?

(A pause.)

PRESTON: Do you miss me?

DAHLIA: Not at all.

PRESTON: Same here.

DAHLIA: We were a big pile of muck.

PRESTON: We were the *Titanic* and Watergate together.

DAHLIA: Worst mistake of my life.

PRESTON: Worse than what's his name? Thorn?

DAHLIA: Burr. Yes, worse than Burr.

PRESTON: Well, you were worse than . . . everybody, too. But . . . Sorry I sent you that dead lizard.

DAHLIA: Sorry I hired someone to beat the shit out of you.

PRESTON: No problem.

DAHLIA: Well. I should go.

PRESTON: Yeah, getting late.

DAHLIA: Bye. Take care.

PRESTON: Good night. You too.

(Silence.)

DAHLIA: Preston, you still there?

PRESTON: Afraid so.

DAHLIA: Just checking.

PRESTON: Admit it, you're not married. You lied.

DAHLIA: I didn't . . . OK, I did. So what?

PRESTON: I lied too.

DAHLIA: When?

PRESTON: When I told you I burned your letters that time. I never did. I sent you the ashes of the Santa Fe *Herald.*

DAHLIA: You kept my letters! Why, to try to blackmail me again?

PRESTON: No. I just like to read them.

DAHLIA:. I want them back. Creep.

PRESTON: Only if you give me back mine.

DAHLIA:. Fine.

> *(Silence.)*

> No. I want to keep them.

PRESTON: You miss me, then!

DAHLIA: Not exactly. I miss your . . . envelopes. Your handwriting. The way you use seventeen words when one will suffice. No one writes me anymore except invitations to these big dumb parties.

PRESTON: Sounds tough.

DAHLIA: I miss your letters.

PRESTON: I could . . . hand-deliver one.

DAHLIA: I don't think so.

PRESTON: OK.

> *(Silence.)*

> All right, then. Guess this is good-bye.

DAHLIA: *(After a beat.)* No.

PRESTON: No? You want — ?

DAHLIA: I want to give you my address. My mailing address — it's just a P.O. Box. Can you send me a letter? I want a letter — a big letter, a real barn-burning rant on the subject of your choice. Be *interesting.* Then we'll see about any further contact.

PRESTON: I'll send you a love letter.

DAHLIA: God no. Immediate disqualification.

PRESTON: So you still hate me?

DAHLIA: I do.

PRESTON: Well I hate you too.

DAHLIA: I've never hated anyone as much as I hate you.

> *(Pause.)*

> Preston?

> Preston are you still there?

> Preston, helloooo!

> Preston?

THE INTERNATIONALIST
Anne Washburn

Dramatic

Lowell, late twenties-early thirties, American; Sara, late twenties-early thirties, not American

Lowell, an American on a business trip to an unspecified foreign country, is met at the airport by a beautiful colleague, Sara, who offers him a lift to his hotel. On the way, they stop for a drink. Here, they are discussing the reason for the flight's mysterious delay.

SARA: *Qui ta me-ad oy fay pempla inst tu dik ni op foi tay.* I got us beers is that alright?

LOWELL: No, that's great. Bring on all of your foreign liquor.

SARA: I got us imports. I'm not providing you with a typical experience am I. Well you've got a week.

LOWELL: *"Oy fay pempla."*

SARA: If you want a beer? *"Oy fay pempla inst foi dik."*

LOWELL: *"Oy fay pempla inst foi dik."* Let me write this down. What about the rest of it.

SARA: *Indink uminting oy fay pempla inst foi dik surt anag.*

LOWELL: OK wait *(He's writing.) "oy fay"*

SARA: *"Indink uminting"*

LOWELL: But you didn't — that's not what you said, is it?

SARA: You don't want to say what I said.

LOWELL: I don't? Why not.

SARA: It's more feminine.

LOWELL: Oh. Oh, that's interesting. Look I hope you don't think I'm a complete jerk. I would have, uh, definitely at least *glanced* at a phrase book but this whole thing happened so quickly. *"Idunk"*

SARA: *"Indink. Uminting. Oy. Fay. Pempla. Inst. Foi. Dik. Surt. Anag."* *(He's writing it down.)*

LOWELL: " . . . *Surt. Anag.*" If I want a beer.

SARA: If you want a beer.

LOWELL: If I want anything else, I'm fucked.

SARA: Or you could say "I'd like a beer." Most people have passable English.

LOWELL: Well that's — yes. Really? Everyone at the company obviously. Your English is very good.

SARA: Oh yes, it's impeccable. Better than yours probably. OK . . .

(The beers have arrived.)

Shall we say, for the purposes of this toast, that you were almost blown up today?

LOWELL: Yes. Excellent. Let's say that.

SARA:. Carpe diem. Carpe diem? Yes. I mix it up with "Buyer beware."

LOWELL: Or "Beware the dog." I did that in college once. I was blind drunk in the middle of the quad in the middle of the night and I was completely gripped by a sense of revelation and I was shouting out at the top of my lungs "Caaaaave Canem! Caaaaave Canem!" Oh my God. Geeky on every level.

SARA: Carpe Diem.

LOWELL: Carpe Diem.

(They toast and drink.)

SARA: Cave Canem.

LOWELL: Cave Canem.

(They toast again and drink.)

So I've been wanting to ask — and then I didn't because I thought is this really American? I want to know what you do.

(She laughs at him, briefly and vigorously.)

I mean at parties, it's got to come up sometime. It can't all be discussions of you know whatever the soul.

SARA: You want to know if you're in some way the boss of me, or if I'm the boss of you.

LOWELL: I do. I do want to know that. I mean is that really? Because don't tell me.

SARA: We say that at parties too.

LOWELL: I was sure of it.

SARA: The difference is that we continue the conversation, regardless of the answer.

LOWELL: OK, no. See that's a prejudice.

SARA: I know, that's what people tell me, they say: "Go to Kansas it's very different there."

LOWELL: That's a . . . a senseless prejudice.

SARA: "It's very different there."

LOWELL: Kansas, oh. What?

SARA: That's the real America. The rest of that behavior doesn't count. Kansas is your — oh what is it.

LOWELL: Aha. I thought your English was impeccable.

SARA: I wouldn't know in mine. Uh, the place where the blood is, on the ground.

LOWELL: Oh the — what?

SARA: The place where the child dies — that's not, that's Greek it's —

LOWELL: One of those kids? In a mine shaft?

SARA: No, it's sort of a concept oh! Jesus. Kansas is your Jesus.

LOWELL: It's —

(He starts laughing.) your English is not impeccable.

SARA: Kansas dies for your sins.

LOWELL: What?!

SARA: Lives for your sins. In Kansas they continue the conversation at a cocktail party, as sincerely as possible, even when they realize that they got stuck with a bum, so that in Hollywood and New York they can just turn and walk away. You know "no no, it's not true, America still has a heart." It's division of Labor. Which is how a nation becomes strong. Here we're a little podunk. We try to each of us take on a lot of human experience, each one of us, so as a result we lose a certain amount of expertise and we all move just a little bit slower.

(Little beat.)

LOWELL: Do I look inevitably American to you? I'm going to develop a rebuttal, by the way, to that last point, it's just a question of time.

SARA: I know you're an American. So I see you as one. I don't know how it would be if walked in, if I saw you sitting here. I think I would — *(Eyeballing him.)* well I would know you were foreign.

LOWELL: Just from looking at me.

SARA: From the way you're sitting. From your presence.

LOWELL: But what if I — yeah, but if I looked as though I knew what I was doing.

(She looks at him appraisingly. She looks at his shoes.)

SARA: If I come in. You're sitting there with your beer. And you don't look confused. *(Beat.)* I think I still know.

LOWELL: Hmmm. And is that interesting here, to be foreign?

(She laughs.)

You know, the accent, is that mysterious.

SARA: But we're speaking English so you don't have an accent. If you were trying to speak my language — people are always more appealing when they're unintelligible.

(He starts to laugh.)

LOWELL: *(He thinks it's an artful misspeak:)* That's witty

SARA: Yes, I know *(She calls out:)* yald ain tant amora koi psam psitay ald imitricikts dor ald tioforian korim tic. Seldis umicktrig orit inial tse hambit orderist il rarin di dam tid norris dimit ona alagoric toyfay int timit oil ald harrick mono borin tam pist i sawan taiya t'noiding lola ka dita hiya fimolla naid he tiad ald terrim kimal doi pimmick ori horind dalna imp porrie gala hondick tibald timiharu. Ai be a toman idat tora abala mot. (She looks back at him.)* I ordered us drinks.

LOWELL: That was ordering drinks?

SARA: There's more than one way to order drinks. OK.

(The waiter lowers a tray with two really very tiny glasses, like half-shot glasses, brimful with viscous red-brown liquid.)

(To the waiter:) Nad urn it orrit imhala tasang al bamadia oritio ib saman. (To Lowell.) You might like this. It's local. Very typical. But we don't usually serve it to tourists. Are you certain you're game?

LOWELL: Absolutely. What is it?

(Gingerly picks up bauble in toast.)

SARA: No I mean really, you're going to have a hard time.

LOWELL: You're joking.

SARA: I'm not.

LOWELL: I'm not at all afraid of a hard time.

SARA: You're not.

LOWELL: No. There's a Latin phrase about that. I forget what. Something about knowledge.

SARA: Well then. Caveat emptor.

LOWELL: Buyer beware.

(As he's raising it to his lips —)

SARA: It's not like a . . . *(Thinking of the word.)* shot, you sip it —

(He does so. His face totally screws up.)

LOWELL: Oh my God.

SARA: Yeah it's —

LOWELL: Oh my God.

SARA: Try to live through it. Try to just —

(His hands are sort of floundering around on the table.)

LOWELL: Water. Water.

SARA: No you can't —

(He calls out to the waiter.)

LOWELL: Water! Water!

SARA: It's a chemical thing. You've got to take another sip — You've got to *(She demonstrates.)* — see? sip. It's counterintuitive.

LOWELL: What?!?

SARA: Take another sip. Take another sip.

LOWELL: Oh no. Water!

SARA: He's not going to bring you water no you've got to, just you've got to, you've got to take another sip. Take another sip. Believe me.

(He does so, his face wrenches up and then clears.)

See?

LOWELL: Oh my God.

SARA: Take another one.

(He does so. It registers.)

LOWELL: That's bizarre.

SARA: Yes it's peculiar.

LOWELL: That's just bizarre.

SARA: You see. Now you take another.

(He takes another tiny sip.)

LOWELL: What *is* this?

SARA: Aren't you glad now that you did it? Take another sip.

LOWELL: It's insane.

SARA: Do you like it?

LOWELL: It's really good.

SARA: You have to suffer first. It's a philosophic beverage.

ITCH
Frederick Stroppel

Comic
Ralph, thirties; Chiffon, thirties

> *Ralph, a writer, has picked up a hooker and taken her to a motel room.*

RALPH: *(Looking around.)* . . . *Wow.* What a great motel room.

CHIFFON: It's all right. Has a nice view of the reservoir.

RALPH: And what is your name, my dear?

CHIFFON: Chiffon.

RALPH: Chiffon? That's a lovely name!

CHIFFON: Yeah.

RALPH: My name is Ralph.

CHIFFON: *(Bored.)* Whatever.

RALPH: Have you been doing this a long time? You look so fresh-faced and vibrant . . .

CHIFFON: Look — can we get started? Because, you know, I'm on the clock right now. You go one minute over the hour, you're paying double.

RALPH: Duly noted.

CHIFFON: Plus I get a break every twenty minutes, regardless of your level of stimulation. It's a union thing.

RALPH: I'm in the Writers Guild myself, so I completely sympathize.

CHIFFON: And I don't do any weird shit. By which I mean to say, if I do any weird shit, it's an extra three hundred.

RALPH: Sounds more than fair.

CHIFFON: And I can't stand on my head, so don't even ask.

RALPH: I'm not planning on making any extraordinary demands. I don't think you'll even break a sweat.

CHIFFON: Yeah, we'll see. *(Beat.)* So — you gonna take your clothes off?

RALPH: No, I don't think so.

CHIFFON: You want me to take my clothes off?

RALPH: Not necessary.

CHIFFON: Do you need to take a pill or something?

RALPH: No, I'm all set.

> *(Beat.)*

CHIFFON: Well, what's it gonna be, tiger? The suspense is fucking killing me.

RALPH: Actually — I have this itch in the middle of my back, and I can't reach it . . . ?

CHIFFON: Uh huh.

RALPH: It's one of those itches, it's really deep, it feels like it's under the skin, absolutely maddening. Right in the center, just beyond my fingertips, taunting, teasing, tantalizing me. I need someone to scratch it.

CHIFFON: You want me to scratch your back?

RALPH: Yes, please.

CHIFFON: That's what you want?

RALPH: Would you mind?

CHIFFON: That's why you hired me?

RALPH: It's driving me crazy.

CHIFFON: *(Shrugs.)* Whatever. *(Ralph sits on the bed. and Chiffon starts scratching his back.)* Like this?

RALPH: Yeah . . . a little higher . . . and to the left . . . Ahh!

CHIFFON: Is that too hard?

RALPH: No, that's . . . oh, yes . . . !

CHIFFON: *(Sexy voice.)* You like that, huh?

RALPH: Oh, yeah . . . Oh, yeah . . .

CHIFFON: That feels good, doesn't it?

RALPH: Wonderful. Won-der-ful . . .

CHIFFON: You want more, don't you?

RALPH: Yes, more, more . . . !

> *(Beat.)*

CHIFFON: You're sure you don't want me to take my shirt off, at least? It's included in the price.

RALPH: No, this is fine . . . a little nail action, please . . . Yeah . . . Ooo . . .

CHIFFON: Or I could talk dirty. I learned a lot of foreign curses from Op Sail.

RALPH: No. no . . . A little more to the center . . . Ah . . . Mmmm . . .

CHIFFON: I got my other hand free, you know; I can just reach down there and . . .

RALPH: Please, no distractions. Just — Ahhh! . . . Ahhhhh! Ecstasy!

(Chiffon continues scratching.)

CHIFFON: *(Getting bored.)* I think I'm gonna put on some music . . .

RALPH: No. don't stop. Keep going!

(Beat.)

CHIFFON: Some weather we're having, huh . . . ?

RALPH: Don't talk! Just scratch!

(Beat.)

CHIFFON: They say El Nino is coming back . . .

RALPH: Will you please be quiet! Please!

(Beat.)

CHIFFON: *(Finally stops scratching.)* This is too fucking boring for me.

RALPH: Excuse me?

CHIFFON: You bring me all the way out here to scratch your back?! You don't think I have better things to do?

RALPH: Hey, I'm paying you, am I not?

CHIFFON: That's beside the point. I'm a professional. I've spent years in the service industry polishing my craft, and I have a certain reputation. You think I'm someone you can just pull in off the street?

RALPH: *(Bewildered.)* Yes.

CHIFFON: Hey, don't break my balls. I have a long list of satisfied customers, I've produced orgasms in all forty-eight contiguous states, and FYI, my pelvis is double-jointed. Incredible, but true. I'm a super star in my field. So when you take up my valuable time for a fucking backrub, it's not only insulting, it's a mockery of everything that I hold sacred.

RALPH: Isn't it your vocation to make people happy?!

CHIFFON: There are limits, pal. I don't mind screwing you or giving you a blow job, but I'm not going to humiliate myself.

RALPH: I'll pay you extra. You can have my watch.

CHIFFON: You're not getting it. I'm a sexual performer! This is not sex! This is something you can do with your wife!

RALPH: *(Quietly.)* No, it isn't. *(Sighs.)* My wife used to scratch my back. Not anymore.

CHIFFON: She's dead?

RALPH: Far from it — she's quite the lively one. She just doesn't want to touch me. She finds me — repulsive.

CHIFFON: Well, she's got a point.

RALPH: Oh, when we were newlyweds, she would scratch my back anywhere, anytime. She took pleasure in it. I would sometimes invent itches, just to give her the chance to employ those elegant fingernails of hers. Oh! but they were long and shapely, like talons, with just a hint of the mandarin about them. Like your nails, my dear. Yes, they remind me of hers.

CHIFFON: *(Self-consciously pleased.)* Do they?

RALPH: But that was in the early days. With time the wild passions faded, the scratch sessions were fewer and farther between. And then one day I came home and she had gotten — a manicure.

CHIFFON: *(Gasps.)* No!

RALPH: *(Nods.)* Every digit, trimmed to the bone. Well, the handwriting was on the wall. One of the great joys of marriage is the option of having any itch scratched with scrupulousness and affection, no questions asked. Take that away, and what's left? Naturally, I sought relief elsewhere. A man has itches, they can't be controlled.

CHIFFON: You could have used a back-scratcher.

RALPH: I also could have rubbed my back up against a pine tree. But I'm a human being! I want to be touched! Sure, it's easy for you, you can walk into any bar or OTB parlor in the world and say "Would you please scratch my itch?" and the boys would be lining up for blocks. But where can I turn? If I approach a stranger on the street and ask to have my back scratched, can I expect anything more than revulsion and ridicule? No, I have to pay a professional sex-monger for a simple act of civility! Do you realize how emasculating that is? How disenfranchising? How crippling to the soul?

CHIFFON: All right, all right, I'll scratch your fucking back. Just stop whining, will ya?

RALPH: It's a hard, hard thing to itch alone. *(She resumes scratching him.)* Ohhh! . . . Ahhhh!

CHIFFON: If your wife won't scratch your back, why don't you leave her?

RALPH: I should, I really should. But she makes fantastic potato pancakes.

CHIFFON: Man, you have some weird fucking priorities.

RALPH: You're missing the spot.

CHIFFON: Right here?

RALPH: No, higher . . .

CHIFFON: Here?

RALPH: No . . . you had it before.

CHIFFON: It's exactly the same spot.

RALPH: No, it isn't.

CHIFFON: It is.

RALPH: Don't you think I know where my own itch is?

CHIFFON: Well, your itch must have moved.

RALPH: Just a little higher . . . Now that's too high! Lower . . . OK, now harder! Aiiee, not that hard! . . .

CHIFFON: *(Walks away.)* All right, that's it!

RALPH: What . . . ?

CHIFFON: *(Gathers up her things.)* No wonder your wife won't touch you. You're a pain in the ass.

RALPH: Where are you going? Don't stop . . .

CHIFFON: I don't need to put up with this bullshit. I'm not married to you.

RALPH: No, please! I'll be good!

CHIFFON: Sure, I know your type. "Higher! Lower! This way! That way! Counterclockwise!" Never satisfied. I'll bet you terrorized that poor woman with your freaky epidermal demands, you needy bastard.

RALPH: That's not true. She loved it. I'm a lovable person.

CHIFFON: You're a monster. I don't even want your money. That reminds me, where's my money?

RALPH: Here, here. Take it all. Just don't leave me.

CHIFFON: I'm supposed to stay here, so I can spend the next hour scratching the dead skin off your spine? Scratch *this,* bozo. Oh, and guess what? *(Wiggles her fingers.)* They're not real. *(She pulls off a nail.)* Press-ons, baby!

RALPH: Oh, Jesus, no!

CHIFFON: That's right. I was faking it. I didn't feel a thing.

RALPH: I don't believe you! I won't!

(He starts to weep.)

CHIFFON: You're pathetic. So long, Itchy.

RALPH: No! Don't go! I'll fuck you! I will!

CHIFFON: Too late now.

(Chiffon exits.)

RALPH: Please, Chiffon! Scratch my back! Scratch my back . . . !

(He crumbles on the floor, distraught, as lights out.)

JUVENILIA
Wendy MacLeod

Seriocomic

Meredith, twenty-one, beautiful; Henry, twenty-one, her boyfriend's best
  friend

*Setting: Henry's dorm room. Meredith discovered that her boyfriend,
Brodie, had slept with someone else when she was home with her
sick mother. To get revenge, she decides to sleep with his best friend
Henry, who has always been sweet on her. Earlier, she maneuvered
Henry's "date," Angie out of the room. Meredith learned of her
mother's death earlier in the evening but hasn't told anyone yet.
Henry was unable to make love to her. Henry and Meredith pull
away from each other.*

HENRY: Well that was weird.

MEREDITH: I've never not made a man hard before.

HENRY: I guess I have a penis with a conscience.

MEREDITH: You do think I'm hot, right?

HENRY: Unbelievably hot.

MEREDITH: Do you ever think about me when you masturbate?

HENRY: You're all I think about.

MEREDITH: What position?

HENRY: It isn't a position exactly. It's more like . . . body parts.

MEREDITH: Uggh.

HENRY: I don't mean like . . . chopping you up.

MEREDITH: *Enough.*

HENRY: It's just you know, when you're with someone, you can feel whether
  or not they love you and if they don't I can't.

MEREDITH: I think I *do* love you . . .

HENRY: You *want* to love me.

MEREDITH: Do you love me?

HENRY: Why does it matter? If you don't love me?

MEREDITH: It matters because I always knew that you loved me, no matter how big a bitch I was, and I thought if somebody as good as Henry can love me, then I can't be all bad, I can't be *evil*.

HENRY: Oh Meredith, people just think you're a bitch because you're a *woman,* you know? Like if Lady Macbeth were a man, she'd be the *hero.* She'd be *Hamlet.*

MEREDITH: Brodie says men want to marry someone nice.

HENRY: Someone nice isn't gonna marry Brodie!

MEREDITH: True.

HENRY: Anyway, Brodie wants to marry you. He talks about it all the time.

MEREDITH: Seriously?

HENRY: Like it's a given.

MEREDITH: I don't think Brodie will ever get married. I don't think Brodie can ever give it up.

HENRY: Some days it feels like the day will never come when somebody will love me. Jenny loved me for awhile and then she stopped, you know? And I could feel the exact moment when it happened.

MEREDITH: Your love-ometer sensed it . . .

HENRY: My weather vane, my divining rod, my cockstand . . .

MEREDITH: Say it with a Long Island accent and you're halfway to Tiffany.

HENRY: Yeah.

MEREDITH: I've been wanting to tell you something for a very long time. Jenny was a complete and total nothing. NYU. Big fucking deal. She's one of 10,000 film majors who's going to end up working in some *video* store or doing *admissions videos.* I saw her on the subway this summer and before I recognized her, you know what flashed through my mind? Complete and total bridge-and-tunnel.

HENRY: Jenny said I completely suck at sex.

MEREDITH: Nice.

HENRY: In an e-mail.

MEREDITH: Angie wasn't complaining.

HENRY: Angie left the room to go find Brodie.

MEREDITH: You are the only one of us worthy of love and it's a mystery to me why you haven't found it.

HENRY: I'd settle for sex.

MEREDITH: No you wouldn't. That's what's so amazing about you.

HENRY: Maybe you could teach me. How to be better at it.

MEREDITH: Your kisses are a little soggy. Go easy on the saliva.

HENRY: OK. What else?

MEREDITH: Nothing. You're fine.

HENRY: I'm "fine"?

MEREDITH: Don't ask *me* to be honest, Henry. You'll be impotent for life.

HENRY: It was that bad?

MEREDITH: No, but . . . your hands are like *paws*. It's like being felt up by someone wearing *baseball mitts.*

HENRY: I have big hands!

MEREDITH: It's not about size, it's about touch. In the Michael Jordan sense.

HENRY: I have no idea what to do with my hands!

MEREDITH: Cradle her face. Caress her breast. Cling to her back. Don't let your arm flap around like a flipper.

HENRY: What else?

MEREDITH: That's it.

HENRY: Really?

MEREDITH: Yeah.

HENRY: So everything was fine except for my hands and my mouth?

MEREDITH: And your penis.

HENRY: Cool.

(An awkward moment. Henry searches for something to say.)

How's your mom?

MEREDITH: Dead.

(Meredith laughs hysterically. Henry doesn't.)

HENRY: Really?

MEREDITH: Really. I found out at dinner. And I was meeting Brodie. So I thought this is good. I'll tell Brodie and he'll comfort me. He'll be my boyfriend for once in his life but of course he wasn't there the prick. He was here. Looking at *porn.*

HENRY: Which he wouldn't have been doing if he knew your mother had died.

MEREDITH: He knew my mother was *sick.*

HENRY: But you never seem to want to talk about it. You always seem to be *handling* it . . .

MEREDITH: What I *seem* like is different from what I *am* like. He's supposed to *know* that.

HENRY: Maybe it takes an entire lifetime to know another human being. Maybe that's what marriage is all about. Maybe people divorce because they're on the verge of really knowing somebody else and it's just too terrifying.

(Beat.)

MEREDITH: Do you mind if I stay here tonight?

HENRY: Sure. I can sleep on the floor.

MEREDITH: No, stay here. Hold me with your big hairy paws.

(Meredith nestles into Henry's arm.)

THE LAST DAYS OF JUDAS ISCARIOT

Stephen Adly Guirgis

Seriocomic
Satan, could be any age; Cunningham, twenties to forties

> *Cunningham, a lawyer, has brought a petition before the court in Purgatory — which looks rather like a Brooklyn courtroom — to try and persuade the court to reopen the case of Judas Iscariot, whom Cunningham thinks has been unfairly treated by history. Here, she has called to the stand none other than Satan.*

CUNNINGHAM: Why do you love God, Mr. Satan?!

SATAN: What's not to love?

CUNNINGHAM: Specifically, Mr. Satan! What specifically do you love about God?

SATAN: I don't know where to begin

CUNNINGHAM: Pick a spot!

SATAN: I love God because He is All Powerful and All Forgiving. I love God because his Justice is perfect. I love God because God loves me.

CUNNINGHAM: God loves you?!

SATAN: Very much. Gift basket at Christmas — Hallmark Greetings on all the major Holidays.

CUNNINGHAM: Stop it! If God loves you, then why did he throw you out of his Kingdom?!

SATAN: He didn't throw me out — I left —

CUNNINGHAM: That's not what it says in the Bible!

SATAN: Yeah, they fudged that part, you're right — but that's because you people really only respond to fear and threat — if they told you straight up that there was no lock to the Gates of Heaven then you'd have no incentive at all to even try to be half-way decent.

CUNNINGHAM: In other words, God lied!

SATAN: God didn't write the Bible — you do know that, right?

CUNNINGHAM: Of course I know that!

SATAN: Then why would you say that God lied?

CUNNINGHAM: Mr. Satan — does God love Judas Iscariot? Yes or No?!

SATAN: God loves everybody.

CUNNINGHAM: And yet Judas is in Hell — so what use is God's Love to Judas if my client is allowed to languish in Damnation?

SATAN: Your client is free to leave whenever he wants to — in fact, I wish he would — I could use the room.

CUNNINGHAM: That's not true and you know it!

SATAN: Look, maybe you should sit down and catch your breath —

CUNNINGHAM: — The real truth is that God's Love for us is Conditional — isn't that right?! You failed to meet God's conditions, and he threw you in the trash! Judas failed — and he's in a catatonic stupor!

SATAN: Your client succumbed to Despair —

CUNNINGHAM: Yes! And if Human Despair is so powerful as to render God powerless over it, then, what does that say about God?! It says one of two things, Mr. Satan: Either God's not All Powerful and therefore useless — or — God's Love is Conditional which renders that Love false and Unworthy! Which one is it?!

SATAN: Cunningham, please don't take this personally, but your father never really loved you or wanted you, right? And the only reason your mother didn't abort you was because she was afraid of scarring — I think she told you that once, didn't she —

CUNNINGHAM: Mr. Satan! —

SATAN: — Just because your parents resented you doesn't mean that God does —

CUNNINGHAM: — Mr. Satan, I asked you a direct question and I am demanding from you a direct answer!

SATAN: The direct answer is that you are completely wrong.

CUNNINGHAM: Is God Powerless or Spiteful — I am ordering you to answer!

SATAN: *(Not unkindly.)* You're powerless and spiteful, Cunningham — not God.

CUNNINGHAM: Your honor, he's not answering!

SATAN: Open your heart to God, Cunningham.

THE MOONLIGHT ROOM
Tristine Skyler

Dramatic
Sal and Joshua, both sixteen

> *Sal and Joshua are two high school students, waiting in a hospital emergency room for word of the fate of an injured friend.*

JOSHUA: *(Casually.)* Should be any minute now.

SAL: What did she say?

JOSHUA: It won't be much longer.

SAL: Did the nurse say anything?

JOSHUA: She asked who I was.

SAL: What did you say?

JOSHUA: I said I'm his brother.

SAL: He's black!

JOSHUA: Don't be so close-minded!

SAL: Then who am I? His white, Irish sister?

JOSHUA: *(The answer.)* You're you.

SAL: *Oh, OK.* So how much longer?

JOSHUA: Soon. *(Pause.)* They don't *want* to keep him here.

SAL: What do you know?

JOSHUA: I'm affiliated with a medical resident here in New York.

SAL: Who?

JOSHUA: My half-stepbrother.

SAL: *Half*-step?

JOSHUA: He and my stepfather do not qualify as *whole* people. There are too many basic human qualities that they're lacking.

SAL: Like?

JOSHUA: Besides humor and charisma? Loyalty and respect. Anyway, he's told me a little bit about working in the ER, the most common types of admissions, procedures, etc., as long as I could bear the conversation. In fact, if you ever meet him, just remember that we're not related.

SAL: Why?

JOSHUA: Because he's incredibly dry, technical, and completely socially inept.

SAL: What do you mean?

JOSHUA: His bedside manner could kill the patient!

SAL: Oh. I get it.

JOSHUA: *(To further prove his point.)* The only placement he could get was in the South Bronx! And they wouldn't even put him in the main hospital. They stuck him in this tiny pediatric emergency room across the Grand Concourse from the main entrance! *(Sal is quiet. There is silence for a few beats.)* Anyway, I'm on a tangent. But this *is* pretty different from *ER*. No one's hooking up and getting busy with each other.

SAL: This isn't television.

JOSHUA: Lightfield auditioned for *Law and Order*.

SAL: Oh yeah?

JOSHUA: Yeah. The part was to play this kid who had just gotten shot. So he went in holding his chest with one of those fake blood pellets.

SAL: Did he get the part?

JOSHUA: No. Actually, they said he stained their carpet. *(Sal laughs a little bit. Trying to entertain her.)* Look I can act. *(He performs a dramatic mock death where he clutches at his throat and then ends up sprawled out on the floor. Sal laughs.)* I should be on that show.

SAL: You wouldn't be allowed. Your GPA's too low.

JOSHUA: So's yours.

SAL: I had substitute teachers.

JOSHUA: I skipped class.

SAL: I was put on the honors track.

JOSHUA: I was put in a peer-counseling consortium.

SAL: *(Casually.)* I have family problems.

JOSHUA: I have attention deficit disorder.

SAL: That's an understatement! *(Josh gets up from the floor. He sits one seat closer to Sal than he was before. There is a pause. A page for a doctor is heard.)*

JOSHUA: We're not going to tell anyone about this.

SAL: Fine.

JOSHUA: Keep it double-down. Lightfield did very well on his PSATs. He'll go to Yale if they give him financial aid.

SAL: I want to go there.

JOSHUA: You have to be more than just smart. You need a *hook*.

SAL: A hook?

JOSHUA: Yeah, a hook. Don't you know what a hook is?

SAL: Not really.

JOSHUA: Like fishing. The hook is like the thing that clinches the deal. You know? Like Lightfield's an actor. And he's black. He's a *black actor.* That's his hook. Like for instance, your hook could be that your mother carpools you to school in Manhattan! *(Sal punches him.)*

SAL: What's your hook? A dime bag?

JOSHUA: *(Proudly.)* I'm an expert chess player.

SAL: Were.

JOSHUA: I won my division. They flew me to Saratoga!

SAL: That was three years ago.

JOSHUA: I'm just waiting to get into the over-eighteens. I got sick of these eleven-year-old freaks in Harlem. I could barely see their heads over the table.

SAL: Sure.

JOSHUA: Do you know who Maurice Ashley is?

SAL: No.

JOSHUA: He's the highest-ranked black player in history. He does Tai Chi before a match. He says chess is intellectual karate. Don't fuck with me. *(Josh starts doing exaggerated, aggressive karate moves, but then slows down into more like Tai Chi.)*

SAL: Yeah right. You quit. Just say it.

JOSHUA: And what sets you apart? *(Sal hesitates.)*

SAL: I won the science fair?

JOSHUA: Oh right. You know, making a DNA model with ping-pong balls and pipe cleaners has been done before!

SAL: Shut up! Mr. Gardino says DNA is the future. He says one day people are going to be able to sell it . . . *(Josh looks at her quizzically for a moment.)*

JOSHUA: Well, if people can sell their DNA, then yours is lying on a blanket on Avenue A next to a rusty clock and some Parliament records.

SAL: I also do volunteering!

JOSHUA: Where?

SAL: At an AIDS clinic.

JOSHUA: What exactly do you do there?

SAL: Office work. I lick envelopes.

JOSHUA: Don't lick the wrong envelope!

SAL: I like it there.

JOSHUA: *(An announcement.)* I'm straight, you know.

SAL: Yes, you like to demonstrate that as much as you can . . .

JOSHUA: . . . none of this bisexual crap like everyone else in school.

SAL: . . . trying to meet that girl tonight . . .

JOSHUA: She was *fine,* that's why.

SAL: She wanted to meet *Lightfield! (Sal pauses. There is silence.)*

JOSHUA: I should call Farland.

SAL: *(Pointed.)* He's a lunatic. *(More silence. Sal looks at Josh. Defensively.)* What?

JOSHUA: Nothing. *(He looks down at the seat next to him.)* Why would Lightfield pass on a girl like that?

SAL: Lightfield's gay.

JOSHUA: You're tripping!

SAL: He doesn't tell you because you're homophobic.

JOSHUA: He's not *gay.* Lightfield isn't a *gay name.*

SAL: *(Incredulously.) It's not?! (Josh doesn't answer. He dips his finger in the peanut butter again.)*

JOSHUA: Do you have any supersize Wonder Bread to go with the peanut butter?

SAL: *(Sarcastically.)* I don't know. Why don't you go look? *(They do more of nothing.)*

JOSHUA: I took Tai Chi once. But of all the martial arts, Maurice excluded, Tai Chi is definitely the one for the gay community.

SAL: What? Why do you say that?

JOSHUA: Maybe because the moves have names like "Grasp the Sparrow's Tail," "Part the Wild Horse's Mane," and "Play the Lute." And the most questionable one is certainly "Repulse the Monkey." *(Sal doesn't respond.)* I get the point of it though, you know, the purpose. It's a practice of attaining peace through balance and continuous motion. It feels like you're moving through water. Like a baby in the womb. *(Sal still doesn't respond They sit in silence for a few beats.)* I'm going to the bathroom. *(He takes off down the hall. Sal sits there for a moment, unsure of what to do. She takes the jar of peanut butter and dips her finger in right where Josh was eating from. She halfheartedly eats a little, then gives up and puts it away. Josh reenters and sits down.)*

SAL: How much longer? I really don't want to have to call my mom.

JOSHUA: The doctor's coming. Chill out.

SAL: I really don't want to have to call her.

JOSHUA: I wouldn't either. She's probably organized a neighborhood search party. With Tupperware. A Tupperware search party. Bring a casserole. And I'm not going to mention the *other* thing.

SAL: Shut up!

JOSHUA: I wouldn't do that to you.

SAL: I appreciate that.

JOSHUA: We have to think about Lightfield right now.

SAL: I agree.

JOSHUA: I don't want to get you upset.

SAL: Thank you.

JOSHUA: So is she still writing letters to the guy from *All My Children?*

SAL: You just said you weren't going to bring that up!

JOSHUA: C'mon.

SAL: When you were expounding upon your theory that my mother appropriates a middle-class suburban lifestyle right in the middle of Manhattan.

JOSHUA: Well, I would say watching a soap opera regularly supports that theory, wouldn't you?! Besides, I wouldn't call Yorkville the middle of Manhattan. It's tangential. It doesn't belong.

SAL: Speak for yourself!

JOSHUA: So is she still writing letters?

SAL: *(Does not want to talk about it.)* She did that once, OK? And it's not like it was fan mail. They met at a bookstore.

JOSHUA: Oh.

SAL: And — besides, that was a good thing. At least she was out. She bought a photo album that day, and a cookbook. She was happy.

JOSHUA: I was just kidding.

SAL: Just lay off already. I don't want to think about her.

JOSHUA: I'm just teasing!

SAL: I go out at night so I can forget about her. I don't want to think about her face, and her television. I want to enjoy myself. It's bad enough when I get home at night and as soon as I put the key in the door I feel this complete sense of dread in the pit of my stomach. Like the air in my apartment is contaminated and I'm about to breathe it in again. *(There is a silence. A page for a doctor is heard. Josh starts to laugh.)* What's so funny?

JOSHUA: Spray some Glade.

SAL: You're such a jerk.

JOSHUA: I'm just kidding.

SAL: *(Not angry at him, but sad, confiding her frustration to him.)* What do you know? Your mom's with someone. She's happy. My mom barely goes out. She says she'd rather stay home and clean the apartment. I'm not even allowed to have friends over because they'll interfere with her depression. And she doesn't want to wash her hair. Sometimes she goes a whole week. I tell her that if maybe we had people around she would start to feel better. But she doesn't listen. She'll sit there watching *Jeopardy* and bad-mouth my dad. The same speech I've been hearing since he left. On and on and on and on. And then when he comes over to pick me up, she puts on lipstick! She doesn't wash her hair, and she has on the same outfit she's worn for three days, but she puts on lipstick! I swear one night I'm going to go out, and I'm just not going to come home. *(They sit in silence for a few beats. Sal becomes embarrassed.)* I just don't want to have to call her. *(Pause.)* You don't realize how lucky you are. You do whatever you want. You could come home tomorrow and it's fine. I come home tomorrow and I'm on the back of a milk carton.

JOSHUA: Have you been on the back of one yet?

SAL: No.

JOSHUA: So calm down.

NEW YORK WATER
Sam Bobrick

Comic
Linda and Albert, twenties to thirties

> *Linda has put a "romance-wanted" ad in a newspaper. Albert has answered it.*

LINDA: Do you recognize this?

ALBERT: That's the postcard I sent you.

LINDA: *(Reads.)* "Dear P.O. Box Number 7-7-7-7-7-7-7. I am everything you wanted and then some."

ALBERT: I would have written more but there's only so much room on a postcard and I made my sevens too big.

LINDA: It was enough to have the handwriting analyzed.

ALBERT: You did? Why?

LINDA: You have to remember that the picture on the front of this postcard is of the Elephant Man. It would make any normal person a little dubious of the sender. Imagine what it did to me.

ALBERT: Yeah, but it had a gag caption about protecting the earth's ozone layer.

LINDA: Oh. really. I'm sorry, but I didn't get it. *(Looks at front of the card.)* Oh! Oh, yes. I see. Now I get the point it's making. If we don't stop using aerosol sprays we'll all soon look like him. That's very clever.

ALBERT: Yes. Now and then I'm very ecology minded.

LINDA: Of course. That was mentioned in the analysis.

ALBERT: It was?

LINDA: *(Letting him in on something.)* I know a good deal about you Albert Hives. Maybe even more than you'd like to know yourself.

ALBERT: Just from my handwriting?

> *(Intrigued, he unconsciously picks up the lemonade and during the following, drinks it.)*

LINDA: You had a very unhappy childhood.

ALBERT: Well, most kids have an unhappy childhood.

LINDA: You're suspicious of people.

ALBERT: I'm not suspicious. I just don't trust them.

LINDA: You would love to have wild, crazy sex but you realize that's almost impossible for an accountant.

ALBERT: My God, the analysis even told you what I do?

LINDA: Your father was a real asshole, wasn't he?

ALBERT: Yes. Yes, he was.

LINDA: And I'm really sorry about your dog.

ALBERT: Thank you. I was only six when Dad ran him over.

LINDA: You were never allowed to go into the living room with your shoes and as a teenager you were dying to try on women's clothes.

ALBERT: Wow. So far right on target.

LINDA: And for some reason, which he was a bit vague on, you haven't talked to your brother in three years. Oh, look, you drank your lemonade.

ALBERT: Hey, so I did. I wasn't even aware of that. You know, I bet subconsciously, that means I really trust you. Or at least want to trust you.

LINDA: Stay right here. I'll get you another drink.

ALBERT: All right. *(Hands her his empty glass.)* I actually found that musty taste quite refreshing.

(Albert sits down at the very end of the sofa, screams, gets up and pulls out another knife from beneath the cushion that he obviously had missed in his search. Linda takes the knife from him.)

LINDA: Sorry. I think that's the last one. I'll be right back.

(She exits to the kitchen.)

ALBERT: *(Talking to her in the kitchen.)* He's not a nice person.

LINDA: *(Downstage.)* Who?

ALBERT: My brother, Jerry. I always had a problem with him. I don't know if you know how older brothers are, but since we were kids, he was obsessed with getting the best of me. He'd beat me out of comic books, he'd beat me out of baseball cards, he'd beat me out of my allowance . . . As we got older he started beating me out of more important things, shoes, underwear, friends . . . Finally he beat me out of the love of my mother.

LINDA: *(Offstage.)* How did he do that?

ALBERT: He bought her a condo in Florida and pays her fifteen thousand dollars a year not to talk to me.

(Linda enters with a glass of cranberry juice and hands it to Albert.)

LINDA: Here you are.

ALBERT: It's red this time.

LINDA: Yes. It's cranberry juice. It's only a couple days older than the lemonade so it should taste about the same. Besides, the water in the tap is awfully brown today. It looks like tea.

ALBERT: I don't like tea.

LINDA: Then I probably made a good choice with the juice. Tell me more about your brother. He must be doing very well.

ALBERT: Not really. He's just a cab driver.

LINDA: He's Pakistani?

ALBERT: Oh, no. He's American but with some major hang-ups. His need to make me look bad is all consuming. I think it goes back to our childhood. When we were kids my mother always hugged and kissed me and called me her angel.

LINDA: But not Jerry?

ALBERT: No. At the time she said he reminded her too much of my father.

LINDA: Some kids are too overly sensitive.

ALBERT: Apparently he was one of them. Anyway, my finishing college and becoming an accountant didn't help matters. Jerry's resentment grew even though I tried my best to be his friend. I even did his taxes for free up until the year I screwed up and he had to spend six months in jail.

LINDA: It's the old story, you get nothing for nothing.

ALBERT: I tried to explain that to him on visiting days. Anyway, when he came out he was more vindictive than ever. He went to a plastic surgeon and had his whole face reconstructed to look like my mother's first boyfriend.

LINDA: And that did the trick?

ALBERT: My mother dropped me like a hot potato.

LINDA: It must be very painful to have someone you love turn on you.

ALBERT: It was devastating. Do you know what he's doing now? He's so obsessed with making me look small in my mother's eyes he's writing a book and dedicating it to her.

LINDA: He's a writer. I'm impressed.

ALBERT: Well, the idea stinks. It's all about the night he was captured and sexually assaulted by an alien from another planet.

LINDA: Oh, my. That didn't really happen to him, did it?

ALBERT: Who knows? He's such a con-artist you never know what to believe. Anyway, forget Jerry. Let's get back to the important things like you and me. Can you keep a secret?

LINDA: Sometimes.

ALBERT: Up until I walked in here, I sincerely wondered if it was worth going on. I've spent so much of my life living defensively, cautious, alert, I never thought I could ever be intimate with anyone . . . let anyone really know me. And then along came Linda. Someone I feel I can finally relax my guard with. Call me crazy, Linda, but I have a wild hunch that you and I can have a relationship made in heaven.

LINDA: *(Sympathetic.)* Poor Albert. Poor, poor, poor, Albert.

ALBERT: Why poor, poor? Right now I'm the happiest man in the universe.

LINDA: I was worried this would go too far. But there was something in your postcard, a warmth, a genuineness, an innocence that I was helpless to ignore . . . an honesty that possessed me, that drove me to continue with this charade, this fiasco, this deception . . .

ALBERT: *(Fearful.)* You're not a man are you?

LINDA: Of course not. Albert, believe me when I tell you this, but our relationship was doomed from the onset.

ALBERT: No, no, don't say things like that.

LINDA: You see, there was something else the analyst discovered in your handwriting. Something I never dreamed would come up. Something that eventually will turn us one against the other, destroying any chance of happiness we might have had.

ALBERT: No.

LINDA: Yes.

ALBERT: What?

LINDA: The city politic, Albert.

ALBERT: No.

LINDA: Yes. You see, Albert, I am an ultra, altruistic, dedicated Liberal, and you, it seems, you are a lowlife, scum-sucking, piece-of-cat-vomit Conservative.

ALBERT: No!

LINDA: I'm afraid yes!

ALBERT: *(To Heaven.)* Oh God! You giveth and then you taketh away!

LINDA: Oh, Albert, had we only been of different races or religions, I know it would have been semi-smooth sailing for us all the way. But there are too many issues to overcome. Fair housing, the homeless, equal opportunity employment, taxing the piss out of the rich. Slowly, our lives will become entangled with these unsolvable problems, and whatever love and passion there was between us will go right down the crapper.

ALBERT: I knew this city of dangling conversation would end up destroying me. There's entirely too much reading being done here. Look, what if I promise to change?

LINDA: You're an accountant. You're not gifted with that ability.

ALBERT: But I'm not a good accountant. I get bawled out about twice a week.

LINDA: It will never work, Albert. We are who we are. I've learned long ago that it isn't us that molds the city. It's the city that molds us. The necessity to be it, to breathe it. The necessity to eat at *this* year's restaurant, to see *this* year's musical . . . to permit ourselves to live in vermin-infested, high-rent dumps, fearing constantly for our lives. The degradation of having to journey day in and day out, in stinking, reeking, overcrowded public transportation, filled with distraught, miserable, short-tempered, Gothamites, frightened to death to make eye contact with one another, each trying to justify this horrendous existence just for the privilege of being able to walk into the intimidating Metropolitan Museum, two or three times a year and laud the fact that they don't have museums like this in Peoria. It doesn't make sense anymore, Albert. That I know. But it is our heritage and duty to pass it on.

ALBERT: *(In awe. After a beat.)* I can't believe you're only a receptionist. Do you have any idea what heights you might reach if you were more together?

LINDA: I know. Everyone who knows me tells me the same thing.

ALBERT: I'm crushed. I'm absolutely destroyed.

LINDA: Nonsense, Albert. Realistically speaking this experience will be extremely beneficial for both of us.

ALBERT: I'm sorry but I can't see how.

LINDA: Eventually we're bound to meet someone we're compatible with. This was wonderful practice. Trust me. I have good instincts. I'm very seldom wrong most of the time.

ALBERT: No! No! I refuse to give you up, Linda.

LINDA: It's not your choice, Albert. Not as long as we live in this metropolis of insane passions and overwhelming mental discomfort.

ALBERT: *(With great difficulty.)* Then that's the answer. We'll leave.

LINDA: Leave? Leave New York? What would we do for . . . culture?

ALBERT: Linda, let's face it. If we stay here *I'll* never be anything more than a below-average accountant and you'll never be anything more than an above-average fruitcake.

LINDA: *(Agreeing.)* True.

ALBERT: Here, we are no more than flower seeds in a dung heap.

LINDA: I know. I know.

ALBERT: Changes need to be made, Linda. We're trapped in a prison of our own making. We have concentrated too long on what's outside of us, rather than what's inside.

LINDA: It's uncanny how often those same thoughts crossed my mind.

ALBERT: Suppressed expression is cerebral enslavement.

LINDA: Once again we're in complete agreement.

ALBERT: And last, but not least, you're nobody till somebody loves you.

LINDA: You're on fire, Albert.

ALBERT: *(Leads her Down Stage Center and indicates the vista.)* Look out there, Linda. Somewhere there's a place where we might actually have a chance to blossom, to expand, to fulfill our true destiny. Tell me you see it.

LINDA: Not yet.

ALBERT: Out there is a land where there are such things as serenity, contentment and meaningful normalcy. Do you see it now, Linda?

LINDA: Not yet.

ALBERT: Out there a new world awaits us, Linda. A world where as husband and wife we can finally discover the real "us" and become who and what we were really meant to be.

LINDA: Excuse me, but in a round-a-bout way did you just ask me to marry you, Albert?

ALBERT: Why, yes, I guess I did.

LINDA: *(Looks at vista with a wide smile.)* I see that place now, Albert. Oh. Albert, I feel the chains of detachment crumbling. I'm breaking loose. I feel stronger and braver. I will go with you anywhere, Albert, even to the ends of the earth if I have to.

ALBERT: Do you mean that, Linda Shoup?

LINDA: I mean that, Albert Hives.

ALBERT: What a remarkable day! To meet the woman of my dreams and get out of this shit hole city forever. Say what you want, it could have only happened in New York!

(They kiss passionately as the lights fade to black.)

NIGHT TRAIN TO BOLINA
Nilo Cruz

Dramatic
Mateo, ten; Clara, eleven

> *This play is set in Latin America during the mid-1980s, during terrible political and military upheaval. Clara and Mateo are two children who have fled their rural village and are trying to survive in "the city."*

> *(In the cemetery. On the scrim a photograph of a cemetery is projected. Mateo flies his kite. The kite is suspended in midair. Clara stands close to him with two large boxes.)*

MATEO: Look at it fly . . . That's how we're going to be, free . . . Free . . . We're going to be free when we escape. *(Waves to the kite.)*

CLARA: Let him go . . . Break the string.

MATEO: No, let him fly higher.

CLARA: Just let him go. *(Mateo cuts the string with his teeth. The kite disappears. They wave to the kite in silence.)*

MATEO: Now he can fly and take the message, then he can go to die where he belongs.

CLARA: I want to go my house.

MATEO: You can't go back, and neither can I. I can't go back. I told you my sister Flora heard me talk in my sleep last night. She heard me talk about our escape. That's why Mama tied my leg to the kitchen table, 'cause Flora told Mama I was talking in my sleep about going to the city. I cut the rope with my teeth. Ha! They thought I couldn't get away. Let's go play with the dead people. This is going to be the last time we play with them, then they'll never see us again. Come on! Let's play pretend. I'll be the man who died in October. You be the woman who died in July. You remember the photograph on her tomb? Let's go look for her.

CLARA: No.

MATEO: You don't like her? You can be another dead woman, if you want. How about the woman who died in 1949? You remember the picture on her tomb? What was her name?

CLARA: Rrrita.

MATEO: Come on . . . You pretend to be Rita. I'll pretend to be the man who died in October. *(Reaches for her hand.)* Come on let's go look for their tombs.

CLARA: I'm not going to the city, Mateo.

MATEO: I thought we had it all planned.

Look at me, we jump on the train, I get in this box, you get inside the other box. No one will see us. *(Gets inside the box.)*

CLARA: I'm afraid. In the city there are soldiers. They'll take us away.

MATEO: Nothing's going to happen. When the night train comes, we jump on it. I know which wagon to get on. The one with the luggage. We hide in the boxes . . . Come on . . . In the city we can sell cigarettes. Like my brother, Luis. Five cents each. I know how to do it. We'll make money. And I will buy you a little rug with the money I make. And you can sell fruits and beans on the sidewalk. When I make more money, we can get a table, like the ones in the market. And we can put all the merchandise on top of the table, like real vendors.

CLARA: And where are we going to live?

MATEO: We could live on the church steps. I've seen people living there.

CLARA: I can't go. I made a promise to be good.

MATEO: If you don't come with me I'll die.

CLARA: Don't say that.

MATEO: All of me will break into little pieces. And I'll be dead. Dead! Watch . . . I'll stop breathing. *(Covers his mouth.)*

CLARA: Don't do that! Stop it! . . . *(Mateo continues to hold his breath. He runs away from her. Clara runs after him.)* Stop it . . . You're scaring me . . . Stop it Mateo.

MATEO: If you don't come with me, I'll die . . . If you don't come with me, I'll die . . . *(Runs faster.)*

CLARA: Stop it! You're going to get sick . . . *(Mateo falls to the ground. He pretends to be dead.)* Mateo . . . Mateo . . . Wake up . . . Don't play dead . . . I know you're not dead. *(Mateo doesn't respond.)* Mateo . . . Oh God! Wake up, Mateo! Mateo . . . Please wake up . . . Wake

up!!! Wake up . . . I'll go with you . . . I promise to go with you . . .
Please wake up . . . I promise. *(Mateo opens his eyes.)* You scared me.

MATEO: You promise to go with me?

CLARA: Yes . . . Yes . . . I'll go with you.

MATEO: Tonight.

CLARA: Yes.

MATEO: Good . . . So let's play with the dead people one last time. Come
on . . . Let's play . . . I'm the dead man who died in October. My
name is Paro. My tomb is right there.

CLARA: I'm the dead woman who died in July.

MATEO: Hello!

CLARA: Hello!

MATEO: What's your name?

CLARA: Rita. My tomb is back there. My tomb has an angel with a horn.
He plays music for me.

MATEO: My tomb has a cross and a wreath of laurel leaves. I was a soldier.

CLARA: Soldiers are mean. They kill and steal children.

MATEO: Not me. I was a good soldier.

CLARA: All soldiers are bad. I don't talk to soldiers.

MATEO: *(Runs around looking for another tomb.)* All right, then I'll be this
man, right here.

CLARA: What's your name?

MATEO: I can't read his name. But they call me Pipiolo like my uncle.
What's your name?

CLARA: I'm still Rita. I'm beautiful like her. I was a singer.

MATEO: I was a barber.

CLARA: Would you comb my hair?

MATEO: I lost my comb.

CLARA: Well, find your comb and your scissors. I'm going to sing tonight
and I want my hair combed. See that tomb right there, that's my
stage.

MATEO: I'll charge you twenty-five cents.

CLARA: I don't have any money. I can give you the flowers on my tomb.

MATEO: I want twenty-five cents.

CLARA: I don't have any money. The soldiers stole my money.

MATEO: The soldiers took my comb. Hide. They'll kill you if they find you. *(Both children run around.)* Ay! Ay! My hand hurts. It hurts a lot.

CLARA: Let me look at it. *(Clara unbinds the bandage.)*

MATEO: Ay!

CLARA: Your hand is purple. It's swollen.

MATEO: No, it's not.

CLARA: It's infected.

MATEO: It's not infected.

CLARA: We have to put something on it. Alcohol.

MATEO: No. Leave it like that. There's nothing wrong with it. Leave it like that.

CLARA: Let me wrap it again.

MATEO: In the city you can learn to be a nurse. You could work in a hospital and wear a white uniform.

CLARA: Me?

MATEO: Yes. And you can learn to give injections. And you can be my nurse when I get sick. *(Clara kisses him on the forehead. Lights fade to black.)*

PLAY IT AS IT LIES
Granville Wyche Burgess

Seriocomic
Young Cecil and Maria, both seventeen

> *Young Cecil, from South Carolina, has been shipped off to a prep school in New England, because his father wants to discourage his ambition to become a professional golfer. Young Cecil is depressed because it's too cold up North to play much golf. At a Glee Club mixer, he meets Maria, a hot-blooded Yankee girl. During the meeting, he decides that, maybe, the North isn't so bad after all.*

("You've Lost That Loving Feeling" begins playing as a silver ball spins, filling the room with dancing light. Maria enters and looks impatiently around her, moving a little to the music. Young Cecil enters.)

YOUNG CECIL: I'm Cecil.

MARIA: Hi. Maria.

(He continues to stare. She musses her hair.)

YOUNG CECIL: Hey, why'd you mess up your hair?

MARIA: So you wouldn't have to look at me.

YOUNG CECIL: But I like . . .

MARIA: I know, that's the problem. Could we dance?

(She makes little dancing movements. Cecil is silent.)

    "I'd love to, Maria!"

(She drags him into position and they dance silently.)

    Guess what I learned in biology today? *(Since he says nothing, she fills in for him:)* "What, Maria?" Frogs are dumb. "Oh, why?" Because if you put a frog in water and slowly turn up the heat, he'll just swim there till he boils to death. But if you throw a frog into a pot of water that's already boiling, he'll jump right out. "Wow, cool."

(He clamps his hand over her mouth.)

YOUNG CECIL: You'd make a lousy ventriloquist. 'Scuse me. *(He puts her hair back in place, but not very well.)* Why are you smiling?

MARIA: 'Cause you'd make a lousy hairdresser.

(She fixes her hair better, then moves to the punch bowl. Young Cecil follows and pours them some punch.)

YOUNG CECIL: Frogs, huh? You like biology?

MARIA: I love it. I'm going to be a veterinarian some day.

YOUNG CECIL: Hope nobody ever leaves you their pet frog. Why do you like it?

MARIA: *(She sits on the bench:)* It teaches you all about life. Take these frogs. They're just like people. You keep making adjustments, acclimating to ever greater levels of stress, you keep handling things until you wake up one morning and you're cooked. But if you can make yourself test the water every day, your instincts'll tell you whether to stay in or to hop out.

YOUNG CECIL: I've hated biology ever since I learned what female spiders do to their mate after making love.

MARIA: Isn't that great!

YOUNG CECIL: Great?! She bites his head off! I mean, *I* know sometimes the female's left unsatisfied, but that's a mite extreme.

MARIA: *(Laughs:)* Where're you from?

YOUNG CECIL: South Carolina.

MARIA: God, the southern accent was designed to seduce women.

(Young Cecil holds his head in mock fear.)

Don't worry, I won't bite.

(He straightens.)

Yet.

(He asks her to dance. They leave their punch on the bench.)

YOUNG CECIL: Do you like this song? I hate it. Who wants to dance slow to a song about losin' that lovin' feelin'?

MARIA: Don't listen to the words, then.

YOUNG CECIL: I won't.

MARIA: Just concentrate on the feeling.

YOUNG CECIL: I will.

(She moves into his arms.)

MARIA: Like it any better?

YOUNG CECIL: It's growin' on me.

MARIA: So, what do you think of us Yankees?

YOUNG CECIL: I hope some of you give me fleas.

MARIA: Huh?

YOUNG CECIL: Nothin'. I love Yankees like a coon loves cornpone.

MARIA: I take it that means "yes."

YOUNG CECIL: I thought I'd hate leavin' home but I don't. There's so much
more to do up here. I feel like a rooster with the fence knocked down.
I don't even miss golf that much.

MARIA: Golf?

YOUNG CECIL: Don't laugh. Golf can teach you things, too.

MARIA: Is that why you play it, to learn something?

YOUNG CECIL: That's why my daddy plays it. I play it because it's fun.
An' because I'm good at it. You wanna learn all about somebody, play
a round of golf with 'em. *(He goes to pick up their punch.)*

MARIA: Will you play a round with me some time?

YOUNG CECIL: Golf?

MARIA: Whatever.

YOUNG CECIL: Sure. *(He gulps some punch and returns to the tray for more.)*

MARIA: My father says golf's the most fun you can have without taking
your clothes off.

YOUNG CECIL: It's a lot of fun.

MARIA: Sure. But take what we're doing right now. Our clothes are on,
right? *(She snuggles into his arms:)* But which would you rather be
holdin', a putter or me?

(He holds her close.)

Touché, Dad!

YOUNG CECIL: Wanna go outside?

MARIA: It's against the rules.

YOUNG CECIL: Never up, never in.

MARIA: Is that a proposition?

YOUNG CECIL: No! I mean, yes! I'll explain it to you later. The bathroom's
got windows. I'll meet you in the bushes.

MARIA: How southern! Is there a phrase for this?

YOUNG CECIL: I think it's called sap-raisin' time.

MARIA: I'll just powder my . . .

*(She smiles and exits. Young Cecil takes a practice golf swing and lets
out a "Whoop!")*

PLAY IT AS IT LIES
Granville Wyche Burgess

Seriocomic
Cecil and Maria, both twenty-seven

> *Cecil is trying to become a professional golfer. He and Maria, who met while Cecil was in prep school, have been married five years. She has given up her career as a veterinarian to travel with him on tour, but she is tired of playing second fiddle to his obsession with proving his father wrong about his career choice.*

> *(Maria, humming, enters in a bathrobe, carrying high heels and drying her hair with a towel. Cecil is offstage humming "Tattooed Lady" happily.)*

MARIA: Did you have fun tonight? You and your buddies were yucking it up like a couple of teenagers.

CECIL: Must have been the champagne.

MARIA: *(Putting on the heels:)* Will you quit qualifying everything? Just admit you had a good time and leave it at that.

CECIL: *(Yelling happily:)* All right, I had a good time! God, we'd better keep it down, these motel walls are paper thin.

MARIA: I make no promises about the noise factor.
> *(She tosses the towel aside and moves to regard herself in a "mirror.")*

CECIL: You think Mama really has a tattoo? I don't remember one.

MARIA: When's the last time you saw her naked?
> *(She slowly lets the robe fall to the floor, revealing a sexy teddy.)*

CECIL: When I was a little boy, I guess.

MARIA: Maybe she got one after you grew up.

CECIL: *(Entering without his shirt:)* Mama?! She's not the type
> *(He freezes.)*

MARIA: Who knows what uncontrollable urges lurk inside a woman's breast. Like it?

CECIL: Where'd you get it?

MARIA: At Linda's.

CECIL: You said that was a Tupperware party.

MARIA: Meet the Tupperware for today's modern woman! There was a man there selling. . . sexual aids, he called them. We bought him out!

(She gets a golf club.)

CECIL: What're you doin'?

MARIA: You're going to teach me the golf swing.

CECIL: In a motel room?

MARIA: Yep.

CECIL: It's complicated.

MARIA: I'm a graduated doctor, I think I can handle it. Come on, it's time I learned what makes you obsess about this game.

CECIL: *(Kneeling in front of her.)* Well, you grip the club like this. That's it, right hand on top. Now drag the club slowly —

MARIA: Wait a minute, I thought you had to get behind the person.

CECIL: That's only in the movies. Now drag it —

MARIA: I want the movies! Movies! Movies! Movies!

CECIL: All right!

(He gets behind her, reaches around and puts his hands on top of hers on the club.)

Flex your knees.

MARIA: Don't some people have a waggle? To help them relax?

CECIL: Yes.

MARIA: Like this?

(She waggles her rear sensuously against Cecil's groin.)

CECIL: Well, that's not exactly the way Arnold Palmer does it.

MARIA: *(Waggling:)* Did you know the word "to win" has its roots in the Hittite word meaning "to copulate?"

CECIL: I love it when you're intellectual.

MARIA: All right, that's enough work with the swing. Now you're going to show me how to putt — the Italian way! I'm going to lie down on the couch and pretend like I'm a nice soft green, with some flat places, and some undulations, and —

CECIL: Don't . . .

(Cecil puts the club back in the bag.)

MARIA: Oh, goody, are you bringing out your "putter"?

CECIL: Let's go to bed.

MARIA: *(Getting on the floor.)* I kinda wanted to do it on the floor.

CECIL: Don't talk dirty like that. It's not you.

MARIA: You used to love it when I talked dirty.

CECIL: That was before.

MARIA: Before what?

CECIL: We got married.

MARIA: I don't believe it? Who had the glorious Penthouse collection?

CECIL: I threw out my Penthouse collection, remember?

MARIA: I didn't know you threw out your libido along with it.

CECIL: You're my wife now. The next morning I sit down with you an' have coffee, we discuss women's liberation an' lawn mowers an' what kind of Jell-O to buy. It's hard to reconcile the two.

MARIA: That Madonna and the Whore stuff comes with my religion, not yours.

CECIL: Maria, come on, tomorrow is the Masters, probably the biggest day of my life. We had a great time tonight, I'm feelin' really good —

MARIA: That's why I'm wearing this. *(Sits next to him:)* Cecil, honey, it's been so long. I'm trying to make this special.

CECIL: You don't have to. *(Trying to joke.)* Sam Snead says never have sex before a tournament. It's bad for your legs —

MARIA: Will you forget about golf for one fucking minute?!

(Cecil gets his putter.)

Oh, no, you're not running away to daffodil-land this time.

CECIL: Fuck off, Maria! *(He pushes her away.)* Just fuck off.

MARIA: See if you can tune this out, Cecil: You're lacking a certain crucial part of the anatomy, but unfortunately testicles do not spontaneously regenerate! *(Gets her robe and towel:)* I'm leaving, Cecil. It's beginning to boil a little too hot around here and this froggie is jumping out before she's cooked for good.

(She exits.)

CECIL: *(Beat. Then a cry of pain!)* Maria!!!

PURE CONFIDENCE
Carlyle Brown

Seriocomic
Simon and Caroline, twenties, Black

> *Simon and Caroline are slaves in the prewar South. Simon is a gifted jockey. Caroline is a housekeeper for the wife of Simon's owner, the Colonel. Simon is a man who knows what he's worth, and he has big plans, which just might include Caroline.*

CAROLINE: Hey you boy.

SIMON: Are you talking to me girl?

CAROLINE: Yeah, I'm talking to you. The Colonel wants to see you.

SIMON: Oh he do, do he? What he wants to see me for?

CAROLINE: I don't know. He told me to come down here and bring you to him.

SIMON: Well, if the Colonel wants see me he can come down here on the track. He ain't the boss of me.

CAROLINE: Listen to you. You sound like you was free or white or something.

SIMON: I ain't neither one, but I know what I'm worth. So, you can just go back and tell the Colonel to bring his self down here.

CAROLINE: I'm not telling him no such thing. And you ain't the boss of me.

SIMON: You got a lot a sass on you girl, you know that? Do you have any idea who I am?

CAROLINE: Yeah, you Simon Cato, the little man with the big mouth.

SIMON: Little? Little? Who you calling little?

CAROLINE: Don't you see me looking down on you?

SIMON: Well, just be careful you don't find yourself looking up from off the ground.

CAROLINE: I don't even think so. How am I going to let a little man like you knock me down, now you stop fooling around and come on before I have to carry you up there to the Colonel.

SIMON: Carry me? Girl you are the original pistol, you know that? What's your name?

CAROLINE: Caroline.

SIMON: You Mattie's girl?

CAROLINE: Yeah, I'm Miss Mattie's girl.

SIMON: You kind of pretty to be so sassy, you know that?

CAROLINE: You ain't bad looking yourself for a little old short man.

SIMON: I may be short, but I'm hard to handle.

CAROLINE: So they tell me.

SIMON: And little, short, whatever I know you don't know nothing about no man.

CAROLINE: How you know what I know?

SIMON: 'Cause I know your Miss Mattie be working you to death, talking your head off and probably got you sleeping on a cot at the foot of her bed. Even if they'd let you, I know you ain't got no time for no man.

CAROLINE: What I don't got time for is a little old big-mouth man like you.

SIMON: But that's exactly what I'm fixing to give you, if you act nice.

CAROLINE: What?

SIMON: Time Caroline, I'm fixing on giving you some time.

CAROLINE: Humph. . . . Miss Mattie and the Colonel say you want to be free. Is that true?

SIMON: Yeah.

CAROLINE: How you going to that?

SIMON: Why you want to know?

CAROLINE: I don't know. I just do that's all.

SIMON: I'm going to buy myself.

CAROLINE: Buy yourself? You can do that?

SIMON: Yeah, if you got the money and you can get somebody to cut you a deal, you can buy yourself free.

CAROLINE: How you going get money? Where you going to get money from?

SIMON: Can you count?

CAROLINE: Yeah, I can count.

SIMON: Well, look at this.

CAROLINE: A hundred dollars? Where you get all this money from?

SIMON: Got it from off of that mister Dewitt, a bonus for winning this race.

CAROLINE: Gee . . . And once you buy yourself free, then what?

SIMON: Work, keep riding, make money, buy some land, some good blood mares, breed 'em, train 'em, race 'em, live.

CAROLINE: Maybe you ain't so little after all.

SIMON: I'm just small Caroline, there ain't nothing little about me.

PURE CONFIDENCE
Carlyle Brown

Seriocomic
Simon and Caroline, twenties, Black

> *Simon and Caroline are slaves in the prewar South. Simon is a gifted*
> *jockey. Caroline is a housekeeper for the wife of Simon's owner, the*
> *Colonel. Simon is a man who knows what he's worth, and he has*
> *big plans, which just might include Caroline.*

CAROLINE: Simon Cato, how you win that race?

SIMON: Mister Cato if you please.

CAROLINE: Excuse me, Mister Cato, but how you win that race.

SIMON: Well, you see I take my little self on top of my big horse and we
run faster then them other little fellows on top of their big horses,
and then I win. Say, "fascinating mister Cato, fascinating, fascinating"

CAROLINE: Fascinating mister Cato, fascinating . . .

SIMON: No, you need one more fascinating in there . . . There's three . . .
"fascinating mister Cato, fascinating, fascinating."

CAROLINE: Fascinating mister Cato, fascinating, fascinating.

SIMON: Thank-you, thank-you, thank-you . . .

CAROLINE: Simon Cato you ain't nothing if you ain't a fool.

SIMON: I like that.

CAROLINE: Like what?

SIMON: Seeing you laughing. And I like you calling me by my name. So,
how you sneak out from under Miss Mattie's bed tonight?

CAROLINE: I didn't sneak out from under nowhere, I don't sleep in Miss
Mattie's room. I sleep on the back porch. I like taking in the moonshine.

SIMON: You was taking in the moonshine? I been taking in the moonshine too.

CAROLINE: No, I mean the light from the moon. If you lie real still you can feel it touching your skin like the way you feel the sunlight do.

SIMON: Was you naked?

CAROLINE: Nothing you could ever hope to see.

SIMON: I could hope. Let me stand up on this here box so I can look you in your eyes girl.

CAROLINE: So, with all this celebrating, does that mean you going to get to buy yourself free?

SIMON: Yeah Caroline that's what it means.

CAROLINE: I try to think about it sometimes but just don't nothing seems to happen. I can't imagine . . . Free.

SIMON: Caroline tell the truth, you like me don't you?

CAROLINE: You all right.

SIMON: Come on Caroline, I'm serious now.

CAROLINE: Serious about what? Little man I don't know what you talking?

SIMON: "Simon I don't know what you talking about?"

CAROLINE: I don't know what you talking about Simon?

SIMON: Talking about you and me.

CAROLINE: How we get to you and me all of a sudden?

SIMON: Caroline there ain't enough time in life for all of this. Wouldn't you like to do something 'cause it was your own idea better than haven't somebody else's idea telling you what to do all the time? There are niggers out there on this very farm that'll never, never see that idea even in they own minds. God made me little and it come to be a blessing. I'm no slave, 'cause I know what I'm worth and I got it figured down to the penny. We could live Caroline, just live. Wouldn't that be wonderful?

CAROLINE: Yeah.

SIMON: Be with me Caroline

CAROLINE: How can I be with you? I belong to Miss Mattie.

SIMON: I'll buy you.

CAROLINE: Buy me? . . . You mean buy me free?

SIMON: I'll buy you, you be with me. You'll be free.

CAROLINE: I don't know Simon. I don't even really know you.

SIMON: We know this life Caroline. We know this life. There're precious few of us that ever get a chance at something. And when we get one we got to take it. Otherwise, then you really is just a slave. Don't nobody want to be that. Be with me Caroline. I'm going to be free, I'm happy and I want to share it.

CAROLINE: You are some fast-talking little man you know that Simon? Can I catch my breath please?

SIMON: You know very well that at any moment it comes into those white folks minds they could put any nigger they want in front of you and say, "Girl that's your husband." Am I lying?

CAROLINE: No, Simon you're not lying.

SIMON: This time you get to choose, 'cause I'm standing here asking you. Will you be with me?

CAROLINE: I don't know you Simon.

SIMON: Take the chance Caroline. Take a chance on me girl.

THE RETURN TO MORALITY
Jamie Pachino

Seriocomic
Arthur, forties; Beverly, twenties

> *Arthur Kellogg is an author whose book has been drastically mis-*
> *construed by the American public, resulting in a media storm, a vi-*
> *olent incident, and his wife having left him. Arthur is drowning*
> *his sorrows in a bar, where he meets Beverly, much younger and very*
> *beautiful.*

> *(Arthur sits, drinking — mid-forties, university professor, lifelong lib-*
> *eral. Beverly, a very attractive young woman, sits at the end of the bar.*
> *Arthur doesn't notice.)*

BEVERLY: Arthur Kellogg, nee Kellerman. Brilliant mind. Unbelievable
   book. Morons taking it seriously. Hard to comprehend, really. *(Puts*
   her hand out:) Beverly Sapperstein. I'm a huge fan. Can I sit down?

ARTHUR: Oh I'm — you're —

BEVERLY: *(Sitting next to him:)* Insane about your work. Your mind,
   it's — beyond genius. I mean, I'm sure you're mobbed with people
   telling you this all the time.

ARTHUR: No —

BEVERLY: No?

ARTHUR: No, I mean — you'd be surprised.

BEVERLY: God it's perfect.

ARTHUR: It's —?

BEVERLY: The book! Who could've dreamt it up? And to let the American public BELIEVE YOU MEANT IT — sheer brilliance! Total
   courage.

ARTHUR: That's it — that's the thing! Nobody —

BEVERLY: Can we sit down? For a minute?

ARTHUR: You really — ?

BEVERLY: I'd kill myself if I let the opportunity to be with you go by.

(Leading him to a table.)

ARTHUR: *(Unconsciously following:)* About the book? The hoax — seeing through the —

BEVERLY: That they would take it seriously!

ARTHUR: Unbelievable! I thought — overestimating the American public, I guess. But you?

BEVERLY: I saw through it right away. I mean what else could it be?! But everyone kept saying: Bev you're nuts! I just couldn't wrap my mind around it any other way. I kept thinking either I'm the stupidest girl alive — or they have to catch up.

ARTHUR: They have to catch up!

BEVERLY: Even my father — *(Imitating.)* "Right Wing Militia, Bev" . . . "This guy'll run for something soon, mark my words."
(They laugh.)
Can you believe it! He was so sure it was full on propaganda. I can't wait to tell him I was right.

ARTHUR: . . . your father?

BEVERLY: Oh he's this bleeding-heart liberal. Conscientious objector. Runs a charity. God you'd get along perfectly! You have to meet him.

ARTHUR: Well, I —

BEVERLY: How'd you come up with it?

ARTHUR: Oh — well, it just occurred to me the direction we were going in. America, right? And that —

BEVERLY: *(Motioning to the Bartender:)* Exactly —

ARTHUR: — nobody actually listens to what's being said anymore.

BEVERLY: Right!

ARTHUR: On the news — or by their politicians

BEVERLY: *(Taking the drinks:)* Put it on my tab.

ARTHUR: Oh, no — I —

BEVERLY: Keep going.

ARTHUR: Really —

BEVERLY: My pleasure.

ARTHUR: Just you know — how, in the given climate, anyone could get a leg up for a time no matter what kind of —

BEVERLY: Propaganda —

ARTHUR: Yes — and and —

BEVERLY: — brainwashing —

ARTHUR: Yes! And —

BEVERLY: — indoctrination —

ARTHUR: — they were offering. Right. But subtle. Slow and —

BEVERLY: — subliminal.

ARTHUR: Exactly! And then I thought, well how do you show that? How do you — you know, communicate that — and I —

BEVERLY: — came up with the book!

ARTHUR: — came up with the book. *The Return to Morality.*

BEVERLY: Even the title. Sheer Brilliance! Total irony.

ARTHUR: And that's it.

BEVERLY: Wow. I can't believe I'm actually sitting here with you. I really can't.

ARTHUR: *(Stunned:)* Who are you?

BEVERLY: What?

ARTHUR: Where did you come from? Are there more like you at home? *(She laughs.)*
I mean — how stupid. "You from around here?"

BEVERLY: "Come here often?"

ARTHUR: *(Both laughing:)* "Nice girl like you." I mean, you're like this apparition. This Florence Nightingale. I don't believe you actually exist. I drank too much and I'm hallucinating. Who are you really? What do you do?

BEVERLY: I go to school, nearby.

ARTHUR: Oh. School.

BEVERLY: The University.

ARTHUR: You're at — the University?

BEVERLY: Getting my masters.

ARTHUR: Oh. Oh, uh huh. Your masters. That's great. That's really —

BEVERLY: Poly-sci. Plus I write for the school paper.

ARTHUR: Right, of course. Budding reporter. Should I be afraid of you? *(They laugh again.)*

BEVERLY: No tape recorders up my sleeve. *(Opens up her arms, as if to show him.)* You'd make a great story, though.

ARTHUR: Oh sure, A Cautionary Tale, as told to . . .

BEVERLY: *(Helping, gently:)* Beverly. Sapperstein.

ARTHUR: Right. *(Smiles. Pause.)* Wow. You really changed my night here, Beverly.

BEVERLY: I did? Really? I'm glad. It's just, you seemed so sad. And I hope you don't take this the wrong way — but I think you're amazing.

ARTHUR: You're — a godsend.

BEVERLY: I am?

ARTHUR: *(Laughs:)* Oh Jesus, yeah.

(They look at one another.)

BEVERLY: You have a wife, don't you?

ARTHUR: Um . . . she left me. About a month ago.

BEVERLY: Oh God. I'm sorry.

ARTHUR: It's OK.

BEVERLY: No, I'm really — it's just like me, to say something like that. You're probably feeling really low.

ARTHUR: No. I mean. I'm really not.

BEVERLY: Oh.

ARTHUR: Not right now.

(He looks at her, then looks away guiltily.)

BEVERLY: Well, I'm crazy about your *buche.* That's Yiddish. For book.

(Beat.)

ARTHUR: Listen . . . can I buy you one?

BEVERLY: Yeah. You could do that.

ARTHUR: Great. Uh —

(He starts to motion to the Bartender.)

BEVERLY: *(Stands:)* I know just the place.

ARTHUR: Hm?

BEVERLY: I know just the place. For succor. *(Stretches out her hand:)* What's say I interview you and get the real story, huh? Top to bottom. Florence Nightingale wants to take you around the corner. What do you say?

(Beat. Arthur doesn't move.)

BEVERLY: Arthur. Trust me, or don't you?

SCHOOLGIRL FIGURE
Wendy MacLeod

Seriocomic

Jeanine, seventeen, an anorexic obsessive exerciser; The Bradley, seventeen, the prize, mourning his third dead girlfriend

Setting: Jeanine's house, front steps. The Bradley is stopping by Jeanine's house to pick up a book on the way home from his Thai cooking class. He has buried his dead girlfriend Monique today. Jeanine is anxious to seduce him before her rival Renee can because the bylaws state: "She who bones him owns him." She has been misled into thinking that The Bradley likes boyish girls because he's gay. She's spent a lot of time in therapy.

JEANINE: The Bradley!

BRADLEY: Hi Jeanette.

JEANINE: Jeanine.

BRADLEY: Sorry. I'm not really thinking straight. Is my nose still red?

JEANINE: It's a little Yeltsin.

BRADLEY: You got a Kleenex? I can't stop crying all the time.

JEANINE: You must be working through some stuff.

BRADLEY: Naw. I'm just sad. Like I hear a song on the radio, you know, and I think about Monique. She had a really good voice. We went camping once and she sang "Kumbaya". She did all the movements you know. Like the clapping and everything.

JEANINE: What I hear you saying is that that was a very happy memory.

BRADLEY: Yeah, like when I think about it, I get happy and then when I remember she's dead I get all sad.

JEANINE: Was it a very passionate love affair?

BRADLEY: Yeah. Until her periods stopped.

JEANINE: I love when that happens.

BRADLEY: It isn't healthy.

JEANINE: I hate when that happens. It's so unnatural.

BRADLEY: The whole thing is so unnatural, you know? Like Romeo and Juliet. They had a problem, OK. A feud. Fucked-up parents. But there was nothing standing in our way except her disease. Which isn't even a real disease cause it's not like caused by a germ.

JEANINE: What I hear you saying is that you're very angry.

BRADLEY: Yeah.

JEANINE: What I hear you saying is "Yeah."

BRADLEY: I came by to get that book you were telling me about?

JEANINE: *The Dummies Guide to Coping With Loss?*

BRADLEY: I guess.

JEANINE: Or would you rather have *When Super Sad Things Happen to Really Happy People?*

BRADLEY: Whatever. I was just stopping by to have something to do. I never know what to do after the funerals, you know.

(Jeanine raises her hand flirtatiously.)

JEANINE: I know.

BRADLEY: Are you like hitting on me?

JEANINE: I know you've been experiencing some . . . confusion.

BRADLEY: Confusion?

JEANINE: It doesn't matter to me who else you love as long as I'm the only woman.

BRADLEY: Huh?

JEANINE: I need to know that I'm the one. And not Renee . . .

BRADLEY: Who?

JEANINE: The other four.

BRADLEY: With the big head?

JEANINE: Ummhmmmm. Oh look, a bunny!

(They look.)

BRADLEY: I mean you're cute and all but . . .

JEANINE: I know. I'm not a man.

BRADLEY: What?

JEANINE: Maybe you could just pretend I was.

BRADLEY: Why?

JEANINE: To get stimulated.

BRADLEY: Why would I pretend you were a man?

JEANINE: If you were of a different persuasion . . .

BRADLEY: Like gay?

JEANINE: Now I know how Elizabeth Taylor felt. When she loved Monty.

BRADLEY: Monty who?

JEANINE: Clift.

BRADLEY: Didn't he love her back?

JEANINE: He couldn't.

BRADLEY: Montgomery Clift?

JEANINE: Montgomery Clift, James Dean, Tom Cruise . . .

BRADLEY: Tom Cruise? Really?

JEANINE: And now The Bradley.

BRADLEY: Look I'm not gay.

JEANINE: You're not gay?

BRADLEY: No. My cousin's gay.

JEANINE: Everybody at school is saying you're gay.

BRADLEY: Why?

JEANINE: Well you're taking that Thai cooking course . . .

BRADLEY: I didn't want to take shop. I already knew how to make a cutting board in the shape of a pig. But I'm straight!

JEANINE: Prove it.

BRADLEY: Oh man.

JEANINE: Would that really be so awful?

BRADLEY: No but . . .

JEANINE: But what?

BRADLEY: It doesn't feel right. Not on the day of Monique's funeral.

JEANINE: Monique's the past, I'm the present.

(Jeanine moves to kiss The Bradley.)

SECOND
Neal Utterback

Dramatic
John, mid-thirties; T, mid-twenties

> *John has hired T, a prostitute, just to talk. In fact, he intends to*
> *confess his sins, which include being part of a government project*
> *to clone Jesus Christ from blood found on the Shroud of Turin. He*
> *also claims to be immortal, as a result of the cloning process.*

> *(A hotel room. T, a beautiful young woman wearing headphones, en-*
> *ters.)*

T: *(Singing.)* "Santa baby, hurry down the —" *(Removing her headphones.)*
   Oh, Hi. I hate Christmas but I love Christmas music, is that weird?
   I'm T.

JOHN: T?

T: T.

JOHN: Like "a cup of"?

T: Like the letter.

JOHN: Does it stand for anything?

T: No. What do you stand for . . .?

JOHN: John.

T: Right, *John.* Can't beat a classic.

JOHN: How do you mean?

T: You're a "John" . . .

JOHN: Yes . . .?

T: Never mind.

JOHN: You look just like your picture in the/

T: /*Money* before funny.

JOHN: Aren't you afraid I might be a cop?

T: Are you a cop, *John?*

JOHN: No.

T: Didn't think so. It's three hundred for just showing up. Three-fifty if
   you touch me, four hundred if I touch you.

JOHN: You have beautiful hair.

T: It's fake. Four-fifty if you perform oral on me, five hundred if I per form on you.

JOHN: You have sort of, uh, a bedside manner/issue, or —

T: /Five-fifty if you screw me, six hundred if I screw you and an even thou sand for anything involving bodily fluids.

JOHN: I don't usually/

T: /Sure/

JOHN: /Do this. In fact/

T: /It's your first time?

JOHN: You don't believe me?

T: Hey, I'll believe anything you want for the next hour.

JOHN: Is that really an option? You screwing me?

T: It's a surprisingly popular choice. *(Starts to take off her top.)*

JOHN: What if I just want to talk?

T: You're kidding.

JOHN: No, I'm not actually.

T: Dirty?

JOHN: No, just . . . regular.

T: I don't get it — are you gonna whack off while we talk? Or . . .

JOHN: No, there's nothing, um . . . I just want to talk.

T: Is this some Julia Roberts — *Pretty Woman* fetish?

JOHN: No.

T: So, you're not going to buy me things, sweep me off my feet?

JOHN: No.

T: Oh. Then I guess . . . three hundred. Don't try anything.

JOHN: I won't.

T: I'm serious. I know seven ways to kill you and I won't break a sweat.

JOHN: No one's going to die. How do you know seven ways — what one of them?

(T nonchalantly pulls out a knife from her backpack.)

JOHN: Oh.

T: *(Takes out an apple from her backpack.)* I was in the Army. Is this what you wanted to talk about, 'cause the meter's runnin'.

JOHN: Yes, no. So . . . I appreciate you coming . . . Christmas Eve . . . in the storm and all.

T: It's my job.

JOHN: Did you take the train or . . . you were in the Army? I guess not many people ask you to — .

T: More often than I'd like. Mind if I sit? *(She does. She pulls another apple out of her backpack.)* Want an apple?

JOHN: No, thank you.

T: It'll make you smart.

JOHN: Said the serpent.

T: Apple a day, keeps the doctor away.

JOHN: I'm not worried about the doctor.

T: Oh, just take the goddamn apple.

JOHN: I, uh, thank you. *(Takes the apple.)* Why don't you like Christmas?

T: *(Carves and eats her apple.)* I'm allergic to tinsel.

JOHN: That's a joke, right?

T: Well, I thought so, but . . . No, I don't like Christmas.

JOHN: But it's a time of hope and forgiveness, isn't it?

T: Oh, don't get me wrong, it's a brilliant gag. Man has managed to make a buck on everything, what . . . sacred? Death, religion, sex. Did you know that you can actually hire someone over the Internet to pray for you? Brilliant.

JOHN: I didn't know that.

T: Stick with me, kid, I'll learn ya. I do love the winters, though. The way the cold burns like a lover that's a little rough. I read that somewhere. The snow wipes everything clean and then it melts and you can start all over, be someone new.

JOHN: I wish that were true.

T: It is. Or, it is if you *want* it to be. You just choose. If you choose to believe that a virgin magically gave birth in some stable in the middle of the desert then, hey, why not.

JOHN: There are things I tried very hard to believe didn't happen — but they did.

T: You're not trying hard enough.

JOHN: What do you believe?

T: I believe that children are our future. Teach them well and let them lead the way.

JOHN: Really?

T: No, man, it's a song. *(Singing.)* "I believe that children are our future. Teach them well and let them hm hm hm . . . " Hi, where have you been for the last, like, century?

JOHN: Funny you should ask.

T: Did you have your sense of humor surgically removed?

JOHN: It's hard to find things to laugh about.

T: You need to ask Santa for some jokes.

JOHN: You still didn't say why you hate Christmas.

T: I'm actually glad you called.

JOHN: Don't you have family to spend the holidays with?

T: Don't you?

JOHN: No, I don't. Well, not really.

T: Why are you asking so many questions?

JOHN: I think I should get to know you before I spill my guts.

T: Like my mama always said, "Don't spill nothin' you can't wipe up." I think she said that. But I make up memories all the time so . . .

JOHN: And what does your mother think of your career?

T: I was abandoned by my mother, crack whore slut, and left, literally, on the doorstep of a clinic. Only she was stoned and she didn't realize, or who knows, maybe she did, that she had left me at a veterinarian clinic. It's why I'm such an animal. Growl.

JOHN: My God, is that true?

T: Do you want it to be true?

JOHN: Is it?

T: No, my mother's a librarian on Long Island. I'm a compulsive liar. And you are gullible. How old are you?

JOHN: Older.

T: Than what?

JOHN: Than you would think.

T: I don't know, I think a lot.

JOHN: You, now, you're smarter than —

T: You would think?

JOHN: Sorry.

T: I'm a hooker, not an idiot.

JOHN: So, how old are you?

T: You don't want to know.

JOHN: Would I go to jail?

T: You're hiring a prostitute. Either way . . .

JOHN: I see your point.

T: Why are you hiring a prostitute to talk to?

JOHN: Why am I hiring a prostitute to talk to?

T: You have an embarrassingly small penis?

JOHN: I do have an embarrassingly small penis.

T: I was kidding.

JOHN: No, it's OK, I do. But that's not why.

T: That's not why?

JOHN: I believe my immortal soul is in peril.

T: . . . And you *don't* want a blow job?

JOHN: And I think you were there.

T: I was where?

JOHN: So, really . . . how old?

T: Seventeen.

JOHN: Seventeen?

T: I'm kidding. I'm twenty-two.

JOHN: It's just that the truth is important to me.

T: Well, how old are you?

JOHN: Older.

T: Lie.

JOHN: I don't want to lie.

T: I told you I'd believe anything you wanted.

JOHN: But you won't tell me anything I can believe?

T: . . . I'm twenty-six . . . going on thirty. The clothes and everything —
    the hair — makes me look younger.

JOHN: Yes.

T: People will believe pretty much anything you tell them.
    [*(Lauren and Vick enter.)*]

JOHN: Will they?

T: And I can charge more if they think I'm younger.

JOHN: Does that mean I get a rebate?

T: Ha. *(She tosses John her backpack.)* You kill me.

SEVEN RABBITS ON A POLE
John C. Picardi

Dramatic
Q, thirties; Julia, twenties

> Seven Rabbits on a Pole *takes place during the Great Depression,*
> *on a Massachusetts farm owned and operated by an Italian Amer-*
> *ican family. Q is a former factory worker, down on his luck, who*
> *has been hired by Julia's father as a handyman. Julia is a mentally*
> *challenged woman. Here, she comes on to Q.*

(Q takes out his harmonica and plays "Beautiful Dreamer." Julia comes
outside wearing a bathrobe. He stops playing.)

JULIA: Why did you stop?

Q: Hey young lady you should be in bed.

JULIA: Can I try it once, please . . .

Q: Just once. It's late.

(Q hands her the harmonica and she blows into it softly, gently.)

JULIA: That sounds nice. Mr. Q how did you catch them rabbits?

Q: I — I played my harmonica and they came, they came marching to-
wards me . . . like — Like I was the Pied Piper.

JULIA: Lawrence read me that story once . . . You were the Pied
Piper . . . Why did you kill them?

Q: It's just the way life is darling.

JULIA: Do you want to kiss me?

Q: No. Don't say things like that, it's not proper . . . I'll see you in the
morning. Go in now.

JULIA: I have a secret. I want to be your wife. Irene wanted to be Peter's
wife. She told me. I saw them in the barn. Peter was kissing her. All
over . . . here and here . . . Do you like my tits?

Q: No, that's very bad talk.

JULIA: But I have to tell you. Peter was on top of Irene. And he — He

touched Irene's tits and kissed them and it looked nice and soft. —
The way they touched.

Q: Julia this is very bad. Now go to bed.

JULIA: It made me feel nice to watch. Did you ever see that before? —
Naked people kissing and touching?

Q: This kind of talk ain't right for a young lady.

JULIA: I have tits. Like Irene. See? See them.

(She opens her robe and shows Q her breasts.)

Q: No.

JULIA: Will you touch them? — Do you like to look at them?

Q: No, no, don't do that.

JULIA: Scarlett was kissed by Ashley. Should I close my eyes? Should I?
Like this . . . *(She does and goes close to Q, waiting to be kissed.)* Will
you kiss me? Will you?

Q: Young lady this is sinful behavior. Go back in the house.

JULIA: — I love you like Scarlett loved Ashley. And love is when everything tastes good and rainy days are perfect.

Q: I'm going to tell your brothers and your father. They wouldn't like this
at all.

JULIA: But they loved. Papa loved Mama. Irene loved Peter. — Let me
touch you. . . . Why won't you?

Q: You need to go back in the house right now.

JULIA: I want to be with you in the barn. Like Peter and Irene.

Q: Don't say anymore. Go inside.

JULIA: We can take our clothes off and lay on top of each other and move
around each other.

Q: Stop it!

JULIA: I want to see you naked.

Q: JULIA!

JULIA: We can love.

(She begins to open her nightgown more and more.)

Q: Don't do that . . .

JULIA: I want to love you.

Q: Julia . . .

JULIA: Touch me,

Q: I said stop this.

JULIA: See me. My body.

Q: No!

JULIA: Look at me.

Q: Cover yourself.

JULIA: I'm a big girl. I want love. Touch me. Touch me now . . . love me.

   (She slips off her bathrobe and Q is faced with Julia as the lights fade.)

SPYWARE
Kelly Stuart

Dramatic
Woman and Man, thirties

> *A husband and wife are upset because their thirteen-year-old girl
> has been acting oddly.*

(A Man looks at a Woman, holding up a pack of cigarettes.)

WOMAN: Our thirteen-year-old smokes cigarettes.

MAN: Where did you find that?

WOMAN: Her bag.

MAN: Why are you going through her bag.

WOMAN: Because I'm her mother. It's my job to know.

MAN: You don't know she smokes.

WOMAN: Half the cigarettes are gone.

MAN: Maybe she's —

WOMAN: Holding them for somebody else? . . . Are you totally gullible
and clueless and naïve? Have you not noticed the sudden appearance
of mascara and eyeliner ringing her eyes like some cocktail-swigging
raccoon in heat — Her three hours of curling iron effort as if she
were going to the Beirut Disco and not eighth-grade first-period al-
gebra — Have you not noticed she's wearing THONG underwear
which she steals, with her alpha girl pack of mini Britney Spears in
training —

MAN: She's not a — how can you say that. So, what, she wears — thong . . .

WOMAN: I never bought those . . .

MAN: So take them away from her.

WOMAN: I will. I will . . . This is wrong.

MAN: It could have been a gift from her friends.

WOMAN: No. She "jacked" them from Victoria's Secret. She revels in being
a kleptomaniac. She knows that one of us cheated on the other. She
knows either you cheated on me or I cheated on you.

MAN: She told you this? How do you know?

WOMAN: I have my ways to find out.

MAN: Maybe you project.

WOMAN: These are cigarettes, not projections.

(She lights one, smokes. The Man takes one, they both smoke furiously.)

MAN: You were the one who cheated on me.

WOMAN: Should we tell her all that? About Mommy's affair, so it can just be all out in the open?

MAN: You want to tell her about Mr. Big Dick? How you chased him around like a dog. Giving him money, WHEN WE WERE BROKE. Forgetting all about your own child.

WOMAN: Are you talking about you or her, bastard.

MAN: Your child, your child. Idiot bitch.

WOMAN: She knows, probably knows from your screaming.

MAN: I have been careful to scream only outside.

WOMAN: She knows from your cobra-like hissing. Shall we flat out just say, then, how Mommy gave Daddy permission to fuck some sex shop clerk who brags about how she loves anal sex on the Internet, so Daddy would feel better after stealing a disk and reading Mommy's ENTIRE E-MAIL correspondence and diary of three years, although things had been over with that jerk for two solid years, but Daddy had to read it, to memorize and recite every sordid detail, to spit back in my face every private fantasy and humiliation, every fucking private thought I ever had.

MAN: That was to save our relationship.

WOMAN: And did it? And did it save our relationship? Did it? Is this the relationship you'd hoped for?

MAN: You didn't read her diary, did you?

WOMAN: No. Of course not.

MAN: She's just a child. She's innocent. This is not her problem, our relationship should not affect her at all. So you wouldn't read her diary would you as some kind of twisted revenge? Just because I read yours. If you did you're a hypocrite.

WOMAN: No.

MAN: You wouldn't lie to me again would you?

WOMAN: No.

MAN: I wish I could trust you.

WOMAN: You can.

MAN: Then how do you know all those things about her, if you didn't read it in her diary? *(Beat.)* We promised the therapist we would be honest, we promised complete honesty now. Because if you have something to hide . . .

WOMAN: I don't. I don't hide anything.

MAN: Who can you trust if you can't trust your family. You haven't been reading my e-mail have you? I CAN'T read yours now because you've changed your passwords but you HAVE my password, but HAVE YOU BEEN READING IT. Because I REALLY HAVE NOTHING TO HIDE but I would just LIKE TO KNOW. If you read her diary.

WOMAN: I didn't.

MAN: Because then you'd be a hypocrite wouldn't you, if you'd done what you've accused me of doing, if you've done the thing you thought violated you.

(He grabs her violently, digs through her pockets.)

WOMAN: What are you doing? What are you doing.

(Comes out with a notebook. Opens it.)

WOMAN: Blank, every blank page is my obliteration, what I don't say, but I can't be accused of.

MAN: If you read her diary then you are a hypocrite and then you can't accuse me of anything. Did you read her diary or not? Did you or not? Tell me the truth.

WOMAN: Blank. Blank. Blank. Blank.

MAN: You fucking hypocrite.

WOMAN: What if she read your e-mail to me? You leave it sitting right on the desktop, all your vile spewing . . .

MAN: If you read her diary, I will find out.

WOMAN: What if you've installed spymaster software on our computer and reading all my correspondence still, still . . . is that what you've done? Have you done that to me? Because I can't think or speak or write without the fear that every keystroke I make is being recorded and sent to you . . . but we have to deal with the cigarettes and thongs and our daughter because she is really fucked up.

MAN: What if she knew you were reading her diary and wrote those things just to fuck with your head?

WOMAN: She would never do that.

MAN: How do you know.

WOMAN: There is spymaster software on our computer. I've had it scanned. It's on there. You did it.

MAN: I did not. I trust you.

WOMAN: You don't. There is software on my computer.

MAN: Why would you do that, have the disk scanned, what are you trying to hide anyway that you're so afraid I'm going to read.

WOMAN: If you put spymaster software on the disk I'm going to make you pay for that. It shows you don't trust after everything we've said, after everything we've done.

MAN: You're fucking someone. Or you're planning to do it, or maybe you've just been thinking about it.

WOMAN: No. Not at all.

MAN: What if she did it?

WOMAN: Our thirteen-year-old?

MAN: What if she did it.

WOMAN: You're blaming her now?

MAN: Someone is guilty here. Someone is guilty. There is a guilty party.

WOMAN: Yes they are. Someone is guilty alright.

MAN: What if you spy on yourself and you then try to blame me but it backfires because I am blaming our daughter who wrote fake diary entries to fool you.

WOMAN: I would never do that to myself.

MAN: How do you know?

WOMAN: I trust myself. I trust myself. I do, I really do.

MAN: Do you? Well one out of three of us is guilty.

(They take another cigarette each from the pack. Smoke.)

WOMAN: Remember how they burned women alive, and if you didn't burn, it meant you were a witch, and you would have to be killed again, but if you did burn, it meant you were innocent.

MAN: I don't remember, but I've read about it. Yes.

WOMAN: I think that our life is like that.

(She stubs out the cigarette. Exits. The Man gets down on his knees, picks up her cigarette and tears it apart examining it.)

WILL YOU PLEASE SHUT UP?
Dan O'Brien

Comic
Sylvia and Tom, twenties to thirties

> *Tom and Sylvia, formerly a couple, haven't seen each other for quite some time, until they run into each other on the subway.*

SYLVIA: "Tom"?

TOM: Yes?

SYLVIA: I've been meaning to ask you, "all these years":

TOM: What?

SYLVIA: Why do you always do the — the quotes thing?

TOM: I'm sorry?

SYLVIA: You know. The "quotes thing"? With your hands.

TOM: I do that?

SYLVIA: Yeah.

TOM: "I" do the quotes thing?

SYLVIA: There — you just did it! Did you see that? Did you realize that, or was it like a tick or something?

TOM: I'm sorry: I do not do the quotes thing. Occasionally I may say "quote-unquote," when reading aloud from a newspaper perhaps, but I do not do the "thing" with my hands. — *You* do the thing with your hands.

SYLVIA: I do not.

TOM: Always did.

You always did the "thing with your hands."

You've been doing "the thing with your hands" this entire conversation.

SYLVIA: I may do the Thing from time to time, like any (quote-unquote) normal person, but —

TOM: You see — you see?

SYLVIA: I did not — I *"said"* quote-unquote — my fingers were never any-
    where near my head —

TOM: This is not normal behavior, Sylvia, I hope you're aware of that —

SYLVIA: Tom: "normal people" do the "quotes thing" from time to time,
    but YOU do it all the time —

TOM: And it is not the Quotes Thing for your information or the "thing
    with your hands" — anybody who's anybody knows enough to call
    it bunny ears.

    (Beat.)

SYLVIA: Bunny ears.

    Why?

    (Tom shrugs.)

SYLVIA: Why call it "bunny ears"?

TOM: Well just look at yourself.

SYLVIA: . . . Well I don't do this sort of thing normally. Not under "nor-
    mal conditions." And if I do do it, if I have been doing it this af-
    ternoon, it's only because you're here. You bring it out in me. Like
    a rash. That's why we "broke up." And if I occasionally make "bunny
    ears" as a reaction to stress, at least I "do" it around "appropriate
    words." You do it whenever you fucking feel like it, "Tom."

TOM: And this really irritates you.

SYLVIA: It does, yeah. Always has.

TOM: "Always" has.

SYLVIA: "Al-ways."

TOM: Really "gets on your nerves"?

SYLVIA: "It sure as Hell does."

TOM: I'm "sorry," Sylvia, I'll "try" to be "more careful" in the "future" not
    to "get on your —

SYLVIA: STOP IT STOP IT PLEASE GOD JUST STOP IT!

    (A subway stop.)

    (A second or two in silence.)

SYLVIA: *(As if nothing's happened:)* Hey, Tom?

    Sorry about that.

    Sorry about the "STOP IT STOP IT PLEASE GOD STOP IT!"
    thing. I guess it's just a little strange, seeing you after all this time.

    All this Time.

"Time. "

I usually don't think about you, and when I do I like to pretend you're dead.

(Beat.)

I'm a different person now too, Tom. I've been through a Hell of a lot.

TOM: Like what, Sylvia?

SYLVIA: Well:

For starters: I found God.

TOM: *(He means this:)* Really?

SYLVIA: Yeah. And then I lost Him.

TOM: *(He also means this:)* Jeez, that sucks.

SYLVIA: Yeah.

TOM: How did you find Him?

SYLVIA: I read somewhere that people in their twenties either find God or go schizophrenic, and you know how much I hate schizophrenics.

TOM: Sure, who doesn't —

SYLVIA: I mean, they sort of really freak me out —

TOM: Sure, sure —

SYLVIA: You see them at bookstores, near the escalator, standing in front of a cardboard cutout of the universe, saying things like Power will come in the final days when the mother returns to Earth and makes love to the sons of Man —

TOM: Right, I hate that.

SYLVIA: So I decided I'd hedge my bets.

TOM: And find God before you went schizophrenic.

SYLVIA: You think I'm crazy.

TOM: No!

SYLVIA: You do.

TOM: Well, I always thought you were a *little* schizophrenic.

But I understand that need. Wanted to find something, to make some sort of sense.

I just can't believe you found Him, Syl, that's all.

I'm jealous.

SYLVIA: Well let me give you some advice: He's not everything He's cracked
up to be.

TOM: No?

SYLVIA: It was a very one-sided affair.

But in every relationship there always has to be one person who loves
the other person more.

Right?

TOM: Where'd you find Him?

SYLVIA: Who?

TOM: God? Where'd you find God?

SYLVIA: At a bookstore, in front of this cardboard cutout of the uni —

(Subway stop. People on and off.)

And then I lost Him because my sister died. You "remember" Jane?

TOM: You're doing it again.

SYLVIA: What?

TOM: The "thing."

SYLVIA: Am I?

TOM: Jane's dead?

SYLVIA: Oh. Yes.

TOM: God — how?

SYLVIA: Kidneys failed.

TOM: Both kidneys?

SYLVIA: Yeah, if you can believe it.

TOM: Don't those things usually happen one at a time?

SYLVIA: Not in Jane's case. Two kidneys, same day. *Ppphhhhttttt.*

TOM: Wow.

Jane.

I can hardly believe it.

— Really healthy Jane?

SYLVIA: What.

TOM: — What?

SYLVIA: Why'd you say it like that? "Really healthy Jane?"

TOM: I don't know. She was just always sort of "healthy."

SYLVIA: You had the hots for her.

TOM: What? No, I did not have "the hots" for your "healthy" sister
Jane — !

SYLVIA: You would've fucked her if you had the chance —

TOM: Syl, I would not have "fucked" your —

SYLVIA: *"You fucked her"!* Oh my God.

(To the subway car:) He "fucked" my dead sister!

TOM: I did not "have sex" with "your" "dead" "sister."

(To the subway car:) And she was alive, when I knew her.

(As an afterthought:) She was a swimmer!

(A subway stop. People on and off.)

(A few seconds in silence.)

SYLVIA: Well.

I'll just have to, sort of, take your word for it.

And what's a little cheating now five years gone?

And she was a gymnast, for your information, not a "swimmer."

TOM: You feeling all right, Syl?

SYLVIA: "Fine." You?

TOM: "Fine."

Scenes for Two Men

BIG OLE WASHING MACHINE
Stephen Belber

Seriocomic
Mike and Jim, thirties

> *Mike and Jim are two actors. They sit facing out, as though look-*
> *ing into a dressing room mirror in front of them. Mike is slightly,*
> *though only slightly, on the "durable" side of the masculine spec-*
> *trum and of a slightly, if not obvious, non-Anglo ethnicity; Jim is*
> *slightly, though only slightly, and relatively, on the "quainter" end*
> *of the masculine spectrum and, generally, pretty Anglo, ethnically*
> *speaking.*

MIKE: Anyone out there tonight?

JIM: No. *(Beat.)* You?

MIKE: Nope.

> *(Beat; they silently mutter sentences to themselves.)*

JIM: You read that article?

MIKE: Which?

JIM: This morning.

MIKE: On the Kurds?

JIM: No, the . . . ah . . . it was actually about appetite-suppression pills.

MIKE: No way.

JIM: Yeah.

MIKE: Funny. *(Pause:)* Good?

JIM: Stupid. *(Beat; they mutter.)* They're making a pill out of the actual
hormone we secrete after we eat a lot. So that we don't. Won't.

MIKE: Eat so much?

JIM: Yeah. *(Pause.)* It's like more advanced than the stuff that's already out
there . . . which . . . you know, *never* works.

MIKE: *(Pause:)* Cool. *(Beat.)* I've been eating like a goddam cow during
this thing.

JIM: Me too.

MIKE: Really?

JIM: I started eating meat again.

MIKE: I didn't know you didn't.

JIM: Three years.

MIKE: You've been devouring the stuff.

JIM: I had a fucking Whopper Junior for breakfast today.

MIKE: *Really?*

JIM: It was like ecstasy — every bite. Totally intense. Rachel almost puked watching me.

MIKE: She's a vegy?

JIM: Whole nine yards. We both were.

MIKE: Wow.

JIM: Yeah. *(Beat.)* Why, is something up with the Kurds?

MIKE: Yeah.

JIM: Yeah?

MIKE: Yeah. They're completely pissed.

JIM: Really?

MIKE: Totally.

JIM: *(Beat:)* Mike?

MIKE: What?

JIM: *(Pause:)* Are *you* a Kurd?

MIKE: No. *(Pause.)* Why?

JIM: I dunno. I mean . . . you . . .

MIKE: What — ?

JIM: I dunno

MIKE: I have Kurdish tendencies?

JIM: No, yeah — No . . . I just thought that maybe —

MIKE: No, man, Kurds are a whole different ball game. Total Sunni badasses. *(Beat.)* I *wish* I was a Kurd.

JIM: *(Pause — wistful:)* Me too.

MIKE: *(Beat; they mutter.)* They had this guy back in the sixties, Mustafa al-Barzani, he used to ride into Iraqi villages on a horse and just wreak total fucking chaos. *(Beat . . .)* Jim, did Rachel like what I was doing in this?

JIM: Mike, she thought you were awesome.

MIKE: I didn't get that impression.

JIM: She totally did, she's just not good at giving compliments. I have to, like, force her to even tell me I was *decent.*

MIKE: Sorry. I don't mean to . . .

JIM: Don't sweat it, it's really hard what you have to do out there. *(Beat.)* I *did* read an article about this Christian fundamentalist group that's trying to make it illegal for banks to charge interest.

MIKE: Really?

JIM: They think interest is like the epitome of greed and the root of modern-day evil . . . or something. *(Pause.)* It's actually an awesome idea. I mean, I know that Rachel and I would buy a place *pronto* if it had interest free — . . .

MIKE: Loans?

JIM: Yeah . . . *(Beat — brutally earnest:)* But I mean, even more so, reading that made me just want to get the hell out of this country and live somewhere where . . . I dunno, where people have more . . . basic, human compassion and imagination and mutual . . . *involvement* with . . . each other.

MIKE: I hear you, man. *(Beat . . .)* You think you and Rachel'll get married?

JIM: *(Pause:)* I dunno. *(Beat.)* It's a tough call. I care so much, but sometimes I'm not sure what about. *(Beat . . . They mutter.)* You wanna run it?

MIKE: Sure.

(They clear their throats and "prep up." Beat — and they begin:)

JIM: You think she'd mind?

MIKE: No. *(Beat.)* I'm sorry it's not better beer.

JIM: Not a biggie. *(Beat.)* She a good roommate?

MIKE: She's all right. Sucks at doing dishes.

JIM: You guys ever . . . ?

MIKE: No . . . she's . . . totally not my type. She's, like, engaged with the world, fully, and I'm just a stay-home slob.

JIM: Maybe you should get more involved.

MIKE: How?

JIM: I dunno — read the paper, take a walk around a new neighborhood, get on a plane and go somewhere. The world's out there, man, ours for the taking.

MIKE: I think I've watched too much football.

JIM: Fuck football. Everything in moderation.

MIKE: You see that Eagles game?

JIM: I did, but does it matter?

MIKE: Not really.

JIM: That's what I'm saying. You gotta soar, Jeff, that's all there is to it, you gotta soar.

(Beat; Mike leans over, hesitantly, and kisses Jim on the cheek. Jim doesn't react. A moment later, Mike kisses Jim on the lips. It lasts for three seconds, and then Jim pulls away; beat.)

JIM: Wow. *(Pause.)* What the fuck.

MIKE: Yeah.

(Mike leans over and kisses Jim again on the lips; it lasts three seconds and Jim pulls away.)

JIM: What the fuck.

MIKE: Sorry.

JIM: That's not part of the . . .

MIKE: I know, I'm sorry. I just wanted to see where the moment went.

JIM: It's a little weird.

MIKE: I know, I'm sorry. *(Beat.)* Honestly, I didn't mean anything by it. Character study. I was just trying to figure out what they would do if there wasn't always that sound cue right there.

JIM: Fine.

(They turn back to their mirrors; beats.)

MIKE: I know what you're thinking.

JIM: No you don't.

MIKE: Yeah I do, you think I'm like some gay Kurd.

JIM: Are you pissed about that?

MIKE: About what?

JIM: That I thought you were Kurd?

MIKE: Why would I be pissed?

JIM: I don't know, maybe you don't like Kurds.

MIKE: I *told* you I liked them.

JIM: You said you *admire* them but who's to say you're not ethnically predisposed to, like, hating them?

MIKE: Fine — but if I *was* pissed, then why would I kiss you?

JIM: I dunno — because you think you're getting into character!

MIKE: So what does that have to do with the Kurds?

JIM: Nothing!

MIKE: OK then!

JIM: Fine! *(Beat; then suddenly turning to him:)* Here's my thing: I'm just here, trying to serve the piece. As for life — we're all just who we are when no one's looking and none of it really matters so long as we serve up the dish when it counts. What *does* matter is that you don't play games during a line-through.

MIKE: Who's playing games?

JIM: Listen — you know how I am, and if I'm *not* like that then I'm still monogamous with Rachel, so for you to come in here and start extra kissing on our final fucking preview is just weird, dishonest experimentation.

MIKE: Now you're implying shit.

JIM: No I'm not

MIKE: Of course you are, you're calling it extra kissing when I just told you I'm conducting character investigation.

JIM: Fine, then let's kiss. Outside the scene. Seriously, put your money where your mouth is.

MIKE: Jim, I'm not like that.

JIM: Bullshit.

MIKE: I'm sorry, but I'm not —

JIM: Me neither —

MIKE: Fine —

JIM: So then let's just kiss as *us* — two guys having a little kiss —

MIKE: Why?

JIM: To get it out of our system.

MIKE: It's not *in* my system!

JIM: Oh right — you were just practicing how to "soar" —

MIKE: Isn't that what this whole thing's about?

JIM: *You* tell *me.*

(Beat; silence.)

MIKE: Fine.

(Mike leans over and kisses Jim on the lips; it lasts three seconds, Mike pulls back, looking at Jim as if to say, "Call it what you will." Beat.)

MIKE: Should we run the other scene?

JIM: Fine.

(*Beat; they clear throats and prep up. Beat. And then: Jim leans over and kisses Mike full on the lips; it lasts five seconds; Mike pulls away; beat.*)

THE BRIGHTEST LIGHT
Diana Howie

Dramatic
Aaron Burr and Robert Troup, both twenty-four

> *In this scene from* The Brightest Light, *Aaron Burr will do anything to draw his roommate, Robert Troup, into a bit of physical activity as a break from their long night of studying to be lawyers. Both are former soldiers in America's War for Independence. Winter, 1780. An attic garret in the Connecticut countryside.*

> *(Troup is reading, but Burr fell asleep reading. When he starts snoring, Troup shakes him.)*

TROUP: Wake up! you need to finish.
> *(Burr wakes with a start, hitting his sword which is propped up nearby. Inspired by its clanking, he grabs the sword and stands up to practice. His early lines are a bit of spontaneous verse while he "cuts the air." Troup tries to keep reading.)*

BURR: "From the winter, the books/
> And the lawyer Smith!
> Dear sword deliver me."

TROUP: Is the Colonel practicing for yet another season at Valley Forge—

BURR: *(Interrupts.)* "A rain-soaked tent for a bed!
> A rock for his weary head/ —"

TROUP: *(Interrupts.)* Or the first meeting of the local Limerick Society?

BURR: *(With a thrust.) Et la!*
> *(Picking up Troup's sword* and *holding it out to him.)*
> Loser re-enlists?

TROUP: If we are taking a break, I need to work on this letter to Alex.

BURR: "The snow has fallen and melted/
> And fallen again/
> Since you've been writing/
> That sad little letter."

TROUP: This is the second letter!

BURR: "Hello Dear Friend, how's by you/
      I know it can't be very good/
      Since you're still in the Army."

TROUP: I must persuade him to back off from . . . a possible challenge.

BURR: Alexander Hamilton, The Man-of-Desperate-Fortune? or is there another one now —

TROUP: *(Interrupts.)* Does everyone know?

BURR: It's all the talk.

TROUP: I can't seem to get through to him that a gentleman does not challenge a minister
(Hands Burr Alex's latest letter.)

BURR: *(Reads.)* "My dearest Robert. I thank you for the concern voiced in your letter, but I must do everything in my power to stop this heinous lie from spreading 'round the country, even if it means fighting the Reverend Doctor Gordon himself. I cannot live at the caprice of others." You will think of something.

TROUP: What else is there? everyone knows it isn't done, yet he is threatening to do it, I am at a loss for words, I —

BURR: *(Interrupts.)* A new perspective might be helpful.

TROUP: Do you take nothing seriously?!

BURR: Do you need to post your letter tonight? is he that desperate?

TROUP: No.

BURR: Sport with me then.

TROUP: Alex used to be such a stickler for following rules.

BURR: With this war, the rules are being broken all around us.

TROUP: *(Looking at the letter again.)* But pursuing a challenge with a minister? A minister! what *is* Alex thinking??

BURR: A little exercise may be just what you and I both need.
(Urging again with his sword.)
You could pretend to be Alex, and I will be the minister.

TROUP: We will wake up everyone in the house.

BURR: But your friend's reasoning might occur to you if you put yourself in his place.

TROUP: As if they were duelling?

BURR: You are Alex, and I am that slanderous, rumor-mongering, preachy —

TROUP: *(Interrupts.)* I don't see your tip.

BURR: I don't see your sword.

(Takes stance.)

En gard!

TROUP: I have no time for this!

BURR: But we are working on your letter to Alex.

TROUP: *(A prayer, as if to God above.)* Let me win, so this foolhardy youth will go back to the real battle and leave me alone.

BURR: That's my role, the minister!

TROUP: Yes, agreed. You are, then, The Reverend Doctor —

(Has to look at letter again.)

William Gordon. I hear he's about fifty years old.

BURR/AS MINISTER: Fifty! Alex will kill me for sure.

(They commence fencing. Burr pretends he is a doddering incompetent. Troup is not very aggressive.)

BURR: Come on, Robert. Alex has more swagger than that.

TROUP/AS HAMILTON: *(Finally portrays his friend.)* I say Reverend, as good a swordsman as you should have served the patriot cause.

BURR/MINISTER: "They also serve who only stand and wait."

TROUP/HAMILTON: And what exactly, Reverend, are you waiting for?

BURR/MINISTER: The French! they will come! and they will save us! I've had my congregation praying for that knock-kneed Commander of yours for some five years, and that's done no good, so I've turned my prayers to the French Army —

TROUP/HAMILTON: *(Interrupts.)* Talk like that could earn you yet another challenge!

BURR/MINISTER: What? is praying not allowed anymore either?

TROUP/HAMILTON: You insulted our Commander.

BURR/MINISTER: Mister Hamilton

TROUP/HAMILTON: *(Interrupts.)* Colonel. I am *Colonel* Hamilton.

BURR/MINISTER: Yes. Tell me, Colonel, do you not remember that the rules we agree to live by are what holds a society together?

TROUP/HAMILTON: *(Meeting Burr's sword.)* I am following the rules, sir! I challenge you, else I must accept that what you say about me is true!

BURR/MINISTER: Yes, I see, but is there not also a rule for me? are ministers not exempt from a challenge?

TROUP/HAMILTON: I have heard your gossip about me from all quarters, over and over again, repeated in the pubs, in the streets —

BURR/MINISTER: *(Interrupts.)* What was it I said, dear man, that has bothered you so?

TROUP/HAMILTON: Sir! I will not repeat it!

BURR: *(Thrusts* and *Troup falls.)* Et la!

TROUP: Enough already!

> *(Burr stays up, active, ready for more.)*
> You know what's really bothering Alex . . .

BURR: *(Interrupts.)* Being stuck at Headquarters.

TROUP: Exactly! he's not out there fighting.

BURR: Yes! There he is, chained to the desk, drafting our Commander's dinner menus, love letters —

TROUP: *(Interrupts.)* And everyone else's promotion.

BURR: That's it! you found it! the reason you were looking for *and* your response. Alex *is* a victim of desperate fortune. Reputations are made out on the battlefield, and he is stuck inside. He is forced to watch on the sidelines while everyone else achieves their glory.

TROUP: And my response is . . . ?

BURR: "Dear Alex, Reconsider this challenge in light of your current position where everything looks worse than it is. Write immediately to the Reverend, describing the dreariness of your situation, being tethered to Washington, and all that. Assume *that* is what the good Reverend meant by desperate fortune, and offer your apology."

TROUP: Now you know that is *not* what the Reverend meant.

BURR: All Alex has to do is offer an apology.

TROUP: No gentleman can refuse an apology . . .

BURR: The good Reverend Doctor Gordon will be most gracious, I am sure.

TROUP: I'll sleep on it . . . if I ever get to sleep tonight.

> *(Turning back to the books.)*

HORTENSIA AND THE MUSEUM OF DREAMS
Nilo Cruz

Dramatic
Samuel and Basilio, twenties

> *Samuel and Basilio are two Cuban brothers who have met a Cuban*
> *American woman who was sent away from Cuba as a child years*
> *ago to escape Castro's Cuba, and who has recently returned to Cuba*
> *as a grown woman.*

SAMUEL: You think it was stupid of me to give her the fireflies?

BASILIO: No. It's not as bad as giving her a frog . . .

SAMUEL: Well, I don't want her to think I'm retarded. *(Looks in her direction.)* I love her . . . I love her . . .

BASILIO: *(Takes off his shirt.)* Yes, you told me that already . . . I like her, too.

SAMUEL: It's a shame she's married.

BASILIO: *(Uses the shirt to dry his sweat.)* It's hot. Give me a light. *(They sit on the ground smoking. Samuel takes off his shirt. They can see the light coming from her room.)*

SAMUEL: *(Looking in her direction.)* She must be getting ready to go to sleep now. You think she sleeps naked?

BASILIO: In this heat, probably . . .

SAMUEL: When we go to the city, I want you to take me to the whore you told me about.

BASILIO: Which one?

SAMUEL: The one who plays music in her room. [*(Luciana is listening now. She is amused by their conversation and is laughing.)*] Did she play music the whole night?

BASILIO: Yes, boleros . . .

SAMUEL: Was she good?

BASILIO: Like fucking a guitar . . .

SAMUEL: I've never done it to music, only to the mooing of cows and the quacking of chickens in the stable. Sometimes I can't concentrate. It's different with music, isn't it?

BASILIO: Much more . . .

SAMUEL: I bet. You can do it to the rhythm . . . Pin . . . Pan . . . Poon . . . Does she really have men come in and out of the room the whole night?

BASILIO: Many men . . .

SAMUEL: And the music, does it ever stop?

BASILIO: No. It goes on forever . . . She uses the music to drown out the men when they cry from pleasure . . .

SAMUEL: Yeah, Melba likes to scream loud when I do it with her. She scares the cows and chickens in the stable. The whole stable gets going . . . I have to cover her mouth. It's different with whores isn't it?

BASILIO: Yes, they do anything you want.

SAMUEL: And if I want them to pretend to be Luciana Maria . . .

BASILIO: Ah, Luciana Maria . . . I get a hard-on just hearing her name . . . *(He touches himself. They both laugh.)* Should we go for the old hand and think about her?

SAMUEL: If you want. *(They cover their crotch with their shirts and unzip their pants. They begin to touch themselves.)*

BASILIO: You know, they say some men go to the brothels to talk like this . . .

SAMUEL: Like confession?

BASILIO: Yes, and the women listen to their dreams . . . They come to spill their hearts out . . .

SAMUEL: I bet the woman who plays music will charge more if I talk about Luciana Maria.

BASILIO: Ah, that name, Luciana Maria . . .

SAMUEL: It must cost more when you talk about your heart. Do I just go in and tell her to be like Luciana Maria?

BASILIO: Ah, Luciana Maria . . .

SAMUEL: Answer me . . .

BASILIO: Yes, then she'll play a record to make you relax. Then, she'll take your pinga in her hand and dip it in a glass of rum . . .

SAMUEL: *(In shock, stops touching himself.)* What do you mean she's going to put my thing in a glass of rum?

BASILIO: Yeah, in rum.

SAMUEL: What for? Why rum?

BASILIO: Alcohol . . . You know microbes, germs . . . Diseases . . . She's got to disinfect it . . .

SAMUEL: But I'm . . . I've never . . . Will it sting?

BASILIO: Like fire it does. You'll like it. It'll get your pinga all fired up.

SAMUEL: Forget it. You spoiled it for me.

BASILIO: *(Softly.)* Ah, Luciana Maria . . . Luciana Maria . . . Luciana Maria . . . *(Basilio has reached an orgasm.)*

SAMUEL: *(After a pause.)* Did you finish?

BASILIO: *(There was more.)* Luciana Maria . . . Maria . . . Madre Mia . . . Madre Maria . . . *(He slumps down.)*

SAMUEL: *(After a pause.)* I didn't. Would you help me think about her? *(Luciana turns off her light. They look in her direction.)* She's gone to sleep now. Would you help me see her in my mind? Would you do that for me? *(Lights change. Sound of drums.)*

KID-SIMPLE
Jordan Harrison

Comic

Oliver, sixteen; Satyr, thirties

> *Oliver, sixteen, the last virgin in the eleventh grade, is alone in a
> forest. He is on a quest to reclaim the Third Ear, a machine for hear-
> ing sounds that can't be heard. The shape-shifting Mercenary, thir-
> tyish, has been hired to seduce Oliver and derail the quest. In this
> scene, he has taken the shape of a Satyr. Sound of steps approach-
> ing. We also hear a jug of liquid, swaying. Slosh slosh slosh.*

OLIVER: Moll?

SATYR: Hullo, pet.

OLIVER: Moll! Emergency!

SATYR: Out of the reach of hearing, pet. We'd ask her along for a toss,
but it's just us two for tea.
(Sound of sniffing.)

OLIVER: You smell like a stable.
(Sound of vigorous, animal sniffing.)

SATYR: You smell like
clean
young
man.

OLIVER: Your breath is like a saloon.

SATYR: Takes an awful lot to get me cockeyed these days.

OLIVER: Cock — ?

SATYR: Hotsy-totsy, flummoxed, *lubricated.*

OLIVER: You mean drunk?

SATYR: As a skunk.
Have a sip.
Makes you see double and feel single, they say.

OLIVER: I'm questing, so you see it wouldn't *do.*

SATYR: I don't see any quest, I just see a nice young boy-pet in the forest
With nothing to pass his time and I just thought I'd *share*.
A cup of the God, a swig of salvation.

OLIVER: You don't look like salvation.

SATYR: Who's to know until you try?

OLIVER: If I've learned one thing from fairy tales, it's never try *anything* you're offered in a forest.

SATYR: I am nothing so very unknown. I am simply that part of you that wants to run your tongue across the great dark woolly abyss of animal magnetism.

OLIVER: I'm not familiar with that part of myself.

SATYR: No, you're not.
(Ouch. The Satyr's got him there.)

SATYR: A drop, at least.
So sweet you'll wish you were all nose.

OLIVER: Maybe a drop . . .
(The Satyr tips the flask over Oliver.)
(Sound of glug glug glug glug glug glug glug glug glug.)

OLIVER: *(Gasping.)*

SATYR: Good stuff, huh?

OLIVER: It's . . . woodsy.

SATYR: More?

OLIVER: I don't think I really —
(The Satyr tips the flask again. More glug.)

OLIVER: — Should. Ohmigosh. Are those hooves?
(Oliver hiccups.)

SATYR: All the better for dancing clippety-clop to the panpipes.
(Sound of a bar or two on the panpipes.)

OLIVER: Are those — *(Hiccup.)* — horns?

SATYR: All the better for lancing grapes on the highest vine.
(Oliver hiccups.)

SATYR: Nasty case of the hickey-ups. Better have more wine to wash 'em down.
(Oliver drinks. Glug.)

OLIVER: That a tail?

SATYR: All the better for. Hmm.

(Sound of his tail wagging in thought.)

OLIVER: Must be good for — *(Hiccup.)* — something.

SATYR: A tail makes you move different. Like you own the world.

(Sound of the Satyr dancing, accompanying himself on his pipe: He plays the guitar lick from the Stones' "Miss You." Get-it-on music.)

    Now you.

OLIVER: Like this?

SATYR: Looks like Doris Day doing the cakewalk.

    It's all in the pelvis, Elvis. *Move.*

OLIVER: I feel silly.

SATYR: Pretend that it's another time ago

    Bacchus has made the river run wine just because he can.

    You lap at the grapey goodness and

    Soon you're feeling like the fucketeer of the forest

    — What else is wine for, right?

    Soon your groin is barking for fresh kill:

    Cur non tam latera ecfututa [Catullus]

OLIVER: Are you speaking English?

SATYR: *Cur non tam latera ecfututa.*

OLIVER: *Ecfuc-? Ecfut toot?*

SATYR AND OLIVER: *Ecfututa.*

SATYR: *Good.* Here now. Just a touch.

(Sound like a society lady luxuriating in a fur coat.)

OLIVER: *(One slushy slurry sentence.)* I knew it I knew what you are Are you one of those YOU'RE NOT HUMAN are you?

SATYR: *Ecfututa.*

OLIVER: But you chase mostly naiads and draiads and maenads Iheard-mostlyright?

SATYR: Not many of those about the woods any more. Nothing but deers and mooses to keep us company. Anything pink starts to look real nice.

OLIVER *(Guileless and very drunk.)* I'm pink.

SATYR: *(Very close, in his ear.)* I know.

THE LAST DAYS OF JUDAS ISCARIOT
Stephen Adly Guirgis

Seriocomic
Satan, any age; Judas, twenties to thirties

> *A trial has been brought in Purgatory, which looks just like a Brook-
> lyn court room, to examine a petition to reopen the case of Judas Is-
> cariot. Judas: hero, victim or villain? Satan has been called to testify
> about his involvement in Judas' case.*

SATAN: I appeared to Mister Iscariot at Bathsheeba's Bar and Grill shortly
after the night in question. I was actually in town for a guy named
Abdul Mazzi-Hatten, but, he never showed. When I encountered
Mister Iscariot, he appeared to have already taken full advantage of
the Happy Hour.

(Judas crosses to playing area. Satan meets him.)

SATAN: Oh. Hello, friend. How are you this evening?

JUDAS: "How am I this evening?" — what are you, a fuckin' maitre de,
man?

SATAN: I'm Clementine. Clementine of Cappadocia.

JUDAS: Yeah?! Well why don't you go home and fuck your mother, Cappa-
douche-a, OK?!

SATAN: "Doe-sha" — Cappa-doe-sha.

JUDAS: What?'?!!

SATAN: It's cappa-doe-sha.

JUDAS: Well lemme ask you something — cappa-douche-ah — do i look
like someone who gives a flying fuck right now about where the fuck
you're from?!

SATAN: I'm very sorry

JUDAS: Sorry don't mean shit, dick! Take all the "sorrys" in the world, pile 'em one on top of the other, ya know what you got, cappa-douche?! You got a big pile a fuckin' nuthin' is what you got! OK?!

SATAN: You're right.

JUDAS: You wanna do somethin' about it??!!

SATAN: No sir

JUDAS: Then go fuck your mother and leave me the fuck alone!

SATAN: I will. Thanks for the advice.

JUDAS: Hey!!! . . . Where you going?!

SATAN: It seems like you preferred to be alone

JUDAS: Why would I prefer that?! What're you saying: I look like some kinda Lone Wolf? like a fuckin' piranha, bro?

SATAN: Do you mean Pariah?

JUDAS: I mean what I mean. Whaddya —need a light or something?

SATAN: Oh. Thanks.

JUDAS: Like this lighter?

SATAN: Very nice.

JUDAS: I bought it today, man. Expensive shit, but — i got it like that.

SATAN: I can see you're a man of wealth and substance, i admire that.

JUDAS: "Wealth and substance" — don't push it. So, what's your name?

SATAN: . . . Clementine. Clementine of Cappadocia

JUDAS: Clementine, eh? Isn't that a girl's name?

SATAN: Not in Cappadocia.

JUDAS: Well, it is here, bro — you sure you ain't a girl, man?

SATAN: Pretty sure, yeah

JUDAS: I'm Judas, Judas Iscariot — maybe you heard of me?

SATAN: Nah, man — I'm from out of town.

JUDAS: You never heard of me?

SATAN: Nope

JUDAS: You don't get around much, do ya Clementine? So where-abouts you from, man — Egypt?

SATAN: Cappadocia.

JUDAS: That's in Egypt though, right?

SATAN: No — Cappadocia is in cappadocia.

JUDAS: I dig your pyramids, man — and the sphinx? *(To bartender.)* Bartender! Hey! More of that Mesopatanium Wine for my Nubian friend! And some dates and figs too! *(To Satan.)* You smoke Opium, Clam?

SATAN: Clem.

JUDAS: And some opium, bartender — the good stuff!

SATAN: You seem like a man on a mission

JUDAS: Took this girl to a puppet show today, man.

SATAN: Yeah? How was it?

JUDAS: Fuckin' sucked. Puppets are bullshit, ya know?

SATAN: In Cappadocia, we burn puppets!

JUDAS: Well, you people got the right idea over there — that Pharaoh, he's a smart man. Yeah, man. Hey, Clammy — Cheers!

SATAN: Cheers!

JUDAS: Yeah. — Whoa! hey man, thass a nice shirt, what you pay for it?

SATAN: Two pieces of silver

JUDAS: Two pieces of silver? HA!!!! I'll give you five. Here ya go, switch shirts with me.

SATAN: But, I'm rather fond of this shirt

JUDAS: C'mon, man — switch shirts — switch shirts, we're buds now, friends an shit, — I'll let you be my wing man — get you laid, bro!

SATAN: A nice brunette?

JUDAS: Two brunettes and a eunuch! C'mon, strip!

SATAN: Oh OK.

(They switch shirts.)

SATAN: *(To audience.)* He was so drunk, he didn't even notice my unmistakably satanic stench

JUDAS: Yo, i dig this shirt, what is it? silk?

SATAN: From Cappadocia

JUDAS: Fuckin' cappadocian Silk!! Alright!

SATAN: Your shirt is nice too.

JUDAS: Yeah?

SATAN: Yeah.

JUDAS: Wow . . . Thanks, man. That's a nice thing to say. Yeah. Been a while since i heard something nice. That's really nice, bro.
(Beat.)

JUDAS: Hey man, if I told you something corny, would you think that I was, like, a dick?

SATAN: Not at all.

JUDAS: OK . . . I'm kinda mildly afraid of going to hell

SATAN: Why?

JUDAS: Minor incident last night — a miscalculation on my part — nothing serious.

SATAN: Well, one thing I can tell you about Hell: As an eternal destination, it's apparently vastly underrated.

JUDAS: Yeah?

SATAN: And "Hell" is nothing more than the Absence of God, which, if you're looking for a good time, is not at all a bad thing. You wanna play the lute, sing Mary Chapin Carpenter — that's what heaven's for. You wanna rock? Apparently, Hell's the venue.

JUDAS: Are there, like, girls down there?

SATAN: Not many, but I hear they import them from developing nations on weekends . . . But hey, I wouldn't worry about going to Hell.

JUDAS: Even if i did something, perhaps, a little controversial?

SATAN: God understands.

JUDAS: Yeah, but, don't choices have, like, consequences?

SATAN: C'mon, you really think we have a choice?

JUDAS: Well, don't we?

SATAN: OK: Did you pass by that fuckin' disgusting, stinky fuckin' leper on your way in here tonight?

JUDAS: Who? Freddy?

SATAN: "Freddy," yeah: You think *he* had a choice, Freddy, stinkin' it up out there, can't scratch his balls for fear a pullin' out his testes? Huh? And what about what's-his-face from the old days — Job? Don't you think if Job had a choice he woulda been like; "OK, God, enough! I get the fucking point"?!

JUDAS: Yeah but, Job did say that!

SATAN: Yes he did! And what happened next, Judas? God kept right on fucking with him until Job made the only choice available — which was to quietly keep his wrinkly ass-cheeks spread wider than the Red Sea till God got tired of drilling him for oil!

JUDAS: I guess . . . But say . . . Ah never mind

SATAN: What?

JUDAS: Not important

SATAN: C,mon.

JUDAS: OK, Well, say, what if someone were to betray, for example. . . the Messiah —

SATAN: — You mean The Messiah, messiah?

JUDAS: Yeah. Say some idiot had a choice to betray the Messiah or not betray him, and, he chose to betray him?

SATAN: Gee, I couldn't say. Whadda you think?

JUDAS: I'd say the guy's fucked, right?

SATAN: I really couldn't say

JUDAS: C'mon Clams, I'm just askin'.

SATAN: Well, since you asked, i guess I'd say that if this guy —

JUDAS: Cuz this is just some hypo-theoretical guy here —

SATAN: Right. I'd say that if this clown we're talking about betrayed the Messiah, that, probably, *"it would've been better for that man if he had never been born."*

JUDAS: Never been born???!!!

SATAN: Hey — you asked

JUDAS: That's heavy, man. That's a fuckin' heavy trip man, clams.

SATAN: I'm thirsty — how 'bout you?

JUDAS: That's fuckin' really heavy

SATAN: Let's have another round here, Pops! Two barrel's of wine and a hooker menu! *(To Judas.)* You OK, man?

JUDAS: Clams, man, I just realized that I haven't been laid in three years, bro. Can ya believe that — guy like me?

SATAN: Three years?

JUDAS: I wasted my prime, man. And then I wasted my prime after my prime.

SATAN: Well, I think you'll prolly get fucked tonight, bro.

JUDAS: Ya think so

SATAN: Yeah. I'm pretty sure.

JUDAS: I wanna 'nother fuckin' drink. Tonight man, i'm gonna drink this fuckin' bar!

SATAN: Hey. Judas, Lemme ask you something: who is this Jesus of Nazareth guy I've been hearing about?

JUDAS: Jesus of Nazareth?

SATAN: Yeah — I heard he's some kinda somebody

JUDAS: Some kinda somebody?

SATAN: Yeah, that's what I heard.

JUDAS: Aw, Fuck that guy, man — he's a bitch!

THE LAST DAYS OF JUDAS ISCARIOT
Stephen Adly Guirgis

Dramatic
Jesus, of course, thirties; Judas, twenties to thirties

> *A petition has been brought before the court in Purgatory, to reopen*
> *the case of Judas Iscariot. Judas: hero, victim or villain? Judas has*
> *been catatonic with despair in hell. In this final scene of the play,*
> *Jesus appears to him.*

> *(Blackout. A beat. Jesus makes his way to Judas. He speaks to us:)*

JESUS: Right now, I am in Fallujah. I am in Darfur. I am on 63rd and
Park having dinner with Ellen Barkin and Ron Perelman . . . Right
now, I'm on Lafayette and Astor waiting to hit you up for change
so i can get high. I'm taking a walk through the Rose Garden with
George Bush. I'm helping Donald Rumsfeld get a good night's
sleep . . . I was in that cave with Osama, and on that plane with Mo-
hammed Atta . . . And what I want you to *know* is that your work
has barely begun. And what I want you to *trust* is the efficacy of Di-
vine Love if practiced consciously. And what I need you to *believe*
is that if you hate who I love that you do not know me at all. And
make no mistake, "Who I Love": is every last one. I *am* every last
one. People ask of me: Where are you? Where are you? . . . Verily I
ask of you to ask yourself: Where are *you?* Where are *you?*

JESUS: Judas.

> *(No response.)*

JESUS: Judas.

> *(Beat.)*

JUDAS: . . . Who's that?

JESUS: Is it ever anybody else, Judas?

> *(Pause.)*

JESUS: I miss you.

JUDAS: Uh-huh.

JESUS: I miss you, Judas

(Jesus lays a hand on him.)

JUDAS: *DON'T FUCKIN' TOUCH ME!*

JESUS: Judas

JUDAS: *I SAID TAKE YOUR FUCKIN' HANDS OFF ME — TAKE 'EM OFF!*

JESUS: I'm sorry. I'm —

JUDAS: *— JUST BACK OFF MY GRILL, MAN! BACK OFF!*

JESUS: I'm sorry.

JUDAS: *BACK OFF MORE!*

JESUS: I'm sorry.

(Pause.)

JESUS: Judas: If a thousand strangers spit on me and kick me as they pass, I will smile. But if the brother of my heart gives me only a passing hard look, then Judas — I will not sleep that night, nor sleep — at all — till he will let me love him again.

JUDAS: *NO!!*

JESUS: No, what?

JUDAS: No more fuckin' fortune cookies, that's what! You wanna say something, i can't stop you — you wanna apologize, fine, apologize and go, just — for once — speak like a normal fuckin' person!

JESUS: I'm not a normal person Judas and I'm not here to apologize. I am who I am and not what you demand me to be. I'm always going to be who I am and what I am, and when have you ever heard me deliver my message any differently, Judas? When?

JUDAS: I . . . Just, go away

JESUS: I won't go away.

JUDAS: Well, that'd be a first

JESUS: I have never gone away, Judas . . . Look at me.

(Judas does.)

JESUS: I love you, Judas. And all i want — all i want — is to be not just near you — but WITH you.

JUDAS: Shoulda thought of that before.

JESUS: Before what?

JUDAS: Just get the fuck outta here, OK?

JESUS: Judas —

JUDAS: Don't fuckin' Judas me — *you're not wanted here,* OK, Mister Fuckin' Above It All?!

JESUS: I'm not above it all — I'm right here in it, don't you see that?

JUDAS: *And don't you get that I don't fuckin' care?!*

JESUS: You think your suffering is a one-way street?! It's not! It's the exact opposite of not!

JUDAS: You got a lot of fuckin' nerve —

JESUS: — and you've got no nerve at all! Where's your *heart* in all this, Judas? You think you were with me for any other reason than that?! It was your heart, Judas. You were *all heart.* You were my heart! Don't you know that?!

JUDAS: I'll tell you what I know: I watched you trip over your own dusty feet to heal the sick, the blind, the lame, the unclean — *any two-bit stranger stubbed their fuckin' toe!* When some lowly distant relative— too cheap to buy enough wine for his own fuckin' wedding suddenly runs out of booze — no problem, you just "Presto Change-O" — *and it was fuckin' Miller Time in Ol' Canaan again, wasn't it, bro?! But when I fuckin' needed you — where the fuck were you, huh?!*

JESUS: Judas —

JUDAS: You forgave Peter and bullshit Thomas — you knocked Paul of Tarsus off a horse— you raised Lazarus from the *fuckin' dead*— but me? Me? Your "heart"?! . . . *What about me??!! What about me, Jesus?! Huh?!* You just, you just — I made a mistake! And if that was wrong, then you should have told me! And if a broken heart wasn't sufficient reason to hang, *THEN YOU SHOULD HAVE TOLD ME THAT TOO!*

JESUS: Don't you think . . . that if I knew that it would have changed your mind . . . that I would have?

(Beat.)

JUDAS: All i know is that you broke me unfix-able — and that I'm here . . . And, you wanna know when you delivered your message differently? At the Temple, Jesus — that's when. And you were beautiful there. And you left there three inches taller. And we all saw it. i loved you. That's all i did. And that's the truth. And now I'm here.

JESUS: Judas — What if i were to tell you that you are not here? That you are with me in my Kingdom even now, and that you have been there since the morning of my Ascension and that you have never left?

(Judas spits in Jesus' face.)

JUDAS: That's what I think about you.

(Jesus doesn't wipe it off.)

JESUS: I love you Judas.

(Beat.)

JESUS: I love you.

JUDAS: *Just Stop!*

JESUS: Don't you see me here, Judas?

JUDAS: *I see a lot of things!*

JESUS: You see alotta things?

JUDAS: *That's right!*

JESUS: How about him? Do you see him?

(Satan appears.)

JESUS: Do you know him? Call unto him. Touch him. He is not there. Because he does not exist, Judas. Rather they must conjure him, and still he is but a vapor blown away by a hummingbird's breath. He is false. He is a lie. He is not real. Touch him, Go ahead.

JUDAS: I don't wanna touch him

JESUS: Stand up, Judas.

JUDAS: You know i can't do that!

JESUS: No. What I know — is that you can.

JUDAS: Get the fuck over yourself!

JESUS: Will you feed my lambs, Judas? . . . Will you take care of my little sheep? . . . will you feed my lambs?!

JUDAS: "feed your lambs"

JESUS: You know exactly what I'm asking you.

JUDAS: Go away!

JESUS: If you don't love me, Judas — then you're gonna have to look me in my eyes and say it.

JUDAS: I don't love you.

JESUS: If you don't love me, then why are you here?

JUDAS: Go!

JESUS: Judas! . . . Judas, don't you know what would happen the very instant you got down on your knees?

JUDAS: Why on my knees? They shoulda buried me standing up — cuz I been on my knees my whole life!

JUDAS: You left me

JESUS: I'm right here

JUDAS: I would have never believed that you could have left me.

JESUS: I never left you.

JUDAS: That you didn't love me

JESUS: I do love you.

JUDAS: Why . . . didn't you make me good enough . . . so that you could've loved me?

JESUS: . . . Please take my hands, Judas. Please.

JUDAS: Where are they?

JESUS: Right here.

JUDAS: I can't see them

JESUS: They're right here

JUDAS: *Where are you going?!*

JESUS: I'm right here.

JUDAS: *Don't leave me!*

JESUS: I'm here.

JUDAS: I can't hurt . . .

JESUS: I love you, Judas

JUDAS: I can't . . .

JESUS: Please stay.

JUDAS: I can't hurt . . .

JESUS: Please love me, Judas.

JUDAS: I can't.

THE LAST SUNDAY IN JUNE
Jonathan Tolins

Dramatic
Tom and Michael, twenties to thirties

> *Tom and Michael are a gay couple. They have hosted a party at their apartment during the Gay Pride March in Greenwich Village (there's a great view from their apartment of the parade). In this, the final scene of the play, they come to realize that, in fact, they are an ex-couple.*

TOM: What am I missing?

MICHAEL: You tell me.

TOM: I'm sorry, Michael. I don't know why I did such stupid things. I love you. But I get distracted. I wish I'd handled it better, the way you did. But I didn't. All I can say is, I'll try to be better. I'll try to . . .

MICHAEL: Stop, please. I didn't hook up with Joe. But there were others.

TOM: Others? When? When I was away?

MICHAEL: And when you weren't.

TOM: Oh. That's why Scott knew the way to the bathroom. *(Michael doesn't answer.)* Well, were you safe? I mean, what did you do exactly . . . ?

MICHAEL: I don't feel comfortable talking about this. Are you really that surprised?

TOM: Yes, I am. I thought you didn't like gay men.

MICHAEL: I don't. I just like having sex with them.

TOM: Well, God, OK, so, we're even. It doesn't mean anything.

MICHAEL: Yes, it does. Don't lie, of course it does. And if it doesn't, it should. Stop being so nice and understanding. It makes it too easy to hurt you. Get mad. I am.

TOM: *(Anger rising.)* What are you mad about?

MICHAEL: That this is it. We've been playing these stupid roles for everyone to see. Maybe if we had talked about it . . .

TOM: We talk.

MICHAEL: No we don't. We, just make jokes and meow.

TOM: *(Letting it out.)* Well, you don't make it very easy, you know, always judging me, always making me the bad guy, when all I do is try to make everybody happy.

MICHAEL: Oh, yes, you're a saint.

TOM: No, but I never pretended to be! Shit, I've been working so hard to please everyone — the partners, my mother, my friends. And the only person who doesn't appreciate it is you! I bought you a house!

MICHAEL: You bought that house for us.

TOM: Because you wanted it and I thought it would make you happy. Which was foolish of me because nothing makes you happy. Why is that? How come I make everybody happy but you?

MICHAEL: Maybe you should just make yourself happy, Tom. *(Beat.)*

TOM: Yeah, maybe I should.

MICHAEL: Don't look to me or anybody else for that.

TOM: "Get my needs met."

MICHAEL: Exactly. Exactly. You know something? This is good.

TOM: It is?

MICHAEL: Definitely. We should have done this a long time ago.

TOM: Yeah, I guess so.

MICHAEL: Things will be much easier now. Now we know. We're "glorified roommates." OK, that's not so bad. I think we'll be OK once we get out of here, you know? Let's just go away. If we could just move to our new house and get away from all of it — the guys, the gym, the plays, the whole parade, we'll be done with it. *(Beat.)* What do you want to do for dinner? I'm thinking Chinese. Will you order? The usual's fine.

(Tom finds a menu in the kitchen. He picks up the phone and dials.)

MICHAEL: That's one thing I'll miss. I'm sure we won't be able to get stuff delivered that fast. Remember the first time we ordered from that place and it seemed like the food arrived before you hung up the phone?

TOM: *(Into phone.)* Hi, Barry it's Tom. Can you please call me as soon as you get inro the office on Monday? I think we need to cancel the inspection. This isn't going to work. I'll explain. Thanks.

(He hangs up.)

MICHAEL: Tom? What the hell are you doing?

TOM: I have to think.

MICHAEL: You want to stay in the apartment and keep throwing rent down the drain?

TOM: I need some time . . .

MICHAEL: Time for what?

TOM: Michael, I love you, but this . . . this isn't . . .

MICHAEL: Oh, God.

TOM: I want more. More than a roommate.

MICHAEL: So does everyone. Look out there. And you know something? Compared to most people, I think we're doing pretty well . . . *(Tom breaks down and sobs.)*

TOM: I'm sorry, Michael. I'm so sorry.

MICHAEL: Don't apologize. *(A touch of panic.)* OK, um, look, do you want us to see someone? How about that? We'll talk to someone.

TOM: I don't know.

MICHAEL: This is not unusual. Really, all couples have problems after seven years. It's the classic, the itch, right? It happens to everyone. In fact, last night in the kitchen, Sherry told me they even went to someone. And now they're doing great. I can get a referral, I'll call her in the morning. Theirs was a straight woman but if you want to go to a gay guy, fine, I'll do that. Every bald guy in Chelsea over forty is a couples therapist. We'll find the right one. There's no reason to panic, we can handle this. Just please, honey, stop crying.

TOM: We haven't had sex with each other in five months.

MICHAEL: We're in a slump, I know that. But, look, we were house hunting, and I had the end of the school year, and you had a bigger caseload. We got very busy . . .

TOM: Five months!

MICHAEL: We lost our connection for a while. We'll get it back.

TOM: I feel you cringe when I go to touch you.

MICHAEL: We'll get it back, Tom.

TOM: I don't think we ever had it.

MICHAEL: Of course we did. We're a good fit, everybody says so.

TOM: That's not the same thing.

MICHAEL: What do you want? Passion? Like you had with James when you were eighteen? Passion fades. Eventually you end up here. God, I can't believe you're going to let that creep ruin everything.

TOM: It's not him. I've had this feeling . . .

MICHAEL: What feeling?

TOM: . . . like it's all passing me by.

MICHAEL: What is? What's out there? Tom, take a good look. Those guys are jealous of us! They've got fun, hot sex, whatever, but we've got a home. And that's the trade-off. It always is.

TOM: It doesn't have to be.

MICHAEL: The house was going to be in both our names.

TOM: We would figure something out.

MICHAEL: How? You're my lawyer.

TOM: You'd get another.

MICHAEL: How would I pay him? I gave up my job. Did you think of that? I'd be out of work and homeless.

TOM: We would figure something out.

MICHAEL: So that's it? Seven years and it's all over when you decide? Because you have "a feeling"? I don't understand why you can't at least try. There's too much good stuff here. I love you, Tom. And you just said you loved me. Now, maybe that's not enough but it's the right place to start. All I'm asking is that you try. Please, Tom. Say you'll try.

(Tom can't. Michael slowly returns to the window.)

MICHAEL: I wanted to go to Pottery Barn.

TOM: I'm sorry.

MICHAEL: Me, too. I'm sorry, too. *(Michael touches his neck and realizes he's still wearing the rainbow beads.)* I forgot I had these on.

MAGGIE MAY
Tom O'Brien

Dramatic
Donny and Charlie, forties

Donny and Charlie wait on the docks for two friends to show up.

DONNY: Jesus, I think I'm a little drunk. Where the hell are they anyway?

CHARLIE: You watch them when they get back. You can always tell when two people have hooked up.

DONNY: How do you tell that?

CHARLIE: You see it in their eyes. It's a glassy look. It's sort of like a crack-head's eyes, but slightly different. And you'll see little looks between them. Quick little glances that they think other people don't notice. And little touches. Like when she gets up to go to the cooler she'll put her hands on his shoulders or touch his waist as she walks behind him. If they have hooked up, you'll just sense a different energy about them. It's a release of the sexual flirtation.

DONNY: What are you talking about? I didn't notice any sexual flirtation.

CHARLIE: That's because you're not perceptive.

DONNY: Yes I am.

CHARLIE: No, you're not. Everybody thinks they're perceptive but you thinking you're perceptive proves that you're not perceptive.

DONNY: How?

CHARLIE: Because you're not perceptive.

DONNY: How do you know?

CHARLIE: It was my business for twenty years.

DONNY: Perception?

CHARLIE: I was a private investigator.

DONNY: I thought you were a venture capitalist?

CHARLIE: That was my cover.

DONNY: Oh, this gets better and better. Where the hell are they? How long does it take to get a bottle of tequila? Did they go to Mexico, for chrissakes?

CHARLIE: Relax, kid. Everything happens slower on the island.

DONNY: I guess I should have read the handbook before I came.

CHARLIE: You a gambling man, Tony?

DONNY: Donny.

CHARLIE: Can I call you Tony?

DONNY: No.

CHARLIE: What do you say you and I make a little wager on whether they hooked up or not?

DONNY: Don't be ridiculous.

CHARLIE: It's an easy bet for you, right? You said she's not here to hook up.

DONNY: She's not.

CHARLIE: All right then. What do you got to lose?

DONNY: Nothing. I don't have anything to lose and I don't have anything to gain and I'm not . . . besides, how would we tell?

CHARLIE: I told you, from the little subtleties.

DONNY: Oh, right. From your private eye days.

CHARLIE: C'mon, let's just bet for fun.

DONNY: I'm not gonna bet.

CHARLIE: C'mon, pussy willow.

DONNY: She's a friend of mine, for godssakes. She's not a racehorse.

CHARLIE:. Gambling just makes life more interesting. It ups the stakes.

DONNY: No . . .

CHARLIE: Gentlemen's bet just for the fun of it.

DONNY: No, those are stupid. If you're gonna bet, you might as well . . . a hundred bucks they didn't even kiss.

CHARLIE: Oh, I like your style, Tony.

DONNY: Donny!

CHARLIE: Right. You're on. Let's smoke on it.

DONNY: What?

CHARLIE: What do you say we smoke some fine Jamaican herb to seal the deal? *(Pulls out a pipe and a bag of weed.)*

DONNY: Oh, this is beautiful. A pot-smoking private eye.

CHARLIE: C'mon, you need to take the edge off.

DONNY: I'm not edgy.

CHARLIE: Yeah.

DONNY: I mean, I'll smoke with you. But I'm not edgy.

CHARLIE: *(Packs the bowl.)* I got this from my Jamaican friends. I gave them a free charter and they supplied me with a trash bag full of this stuff.

(He takes a hit and passes it to Donny.)

CHARLIE: Careful, it's strong.

DONNY: Oh, that tastes nice.

CHARLIE: It's the finest you can get.

DONNY: Holy shit, that's good.

CHARLIE: That's what I'm saying, kid, huh?

DONNY: Yeah.

CHARLIE: That's what I'm saying.

DONNY: Uh huh, yup.

CHARLIE: That don't get old.

DONNY: No, oh that's nice. *(He is in a bit of a stoned haze.)*

CHARLIE: I mean, you're drinking Budweisers and smoking some cheap-ass-back-of-the-school-bus weed. It gets old. But if you drink the finest imported wines, have steak that melts in your mouth, scotch, cigars, this beautiful Jamaican herb. It is happiness. This is it. They don't want to tell you that. But here it is, my friend. Happiness. They don't know. The people writing the self-help books? The "happiness comes from within" bullshit. They don't got access to this stuff. How would they know happiness when they don't even know what the world has to offer? Do I look unhappy? Do I look like I'm search-ing for meaning in life? Like I'm looking for a soul mate to spend my golden years with? Fuck off! They're all golden years. I'm living a golden life. I beat the fucking system, kid.

(Donny is lost in his haze.)

CHARLIE: And then my grandpappy made love to me in an outhouse.

DONNY: What?

CHARLIE: Just seeing if you're still listening,

DONNY: Sorry.

CHARLIE: Thinking about your girl?

DONNY: No.

CHARLIE: Yeah you are.

DONNY: Charlie, I'm not. I'm telling you.

CHARLIE: I been there, kid. I know what you're going through, Don't make decisions based on fear. That's death.

DONNY: I'm not. I . . .

CHARLIE: Listen to me. Here's the deal, OK. There's all these lives out there just floating around waiting for you to live them. You have all these choices to make. Every choice you make splits things off into another parallel universe that's happening simultaneously to your own pathetic reality.

DONNY: What?

CHARLIE: There's two lives in front of you right this second. A fork in the road, shall we say. Two roads diverged in the yellow wood. Which one you gonna take, bubba, huh?

DONNY: I don't know. Wait, what the fuck are you talking about?

CHARLIE: Think about it. Most of the time we're too afraid to live. We say, "I couldn't do that, I couldn't be with her. I don't want to be happy." We talk ourselves out of living. But it's still out there. It's waiting for you. It's happening whether you choose it or not. It's just a question of whether you're gonna go for the ride or sit on the sidelines hopin' and dreamin'. All you have to do is step into it. *(Beat.)* A life unlived is not a life at all.

DONNY: The Tao of Charlie.

CHARLIE: You joke now. But someday you'll realize I was right. Hopin' and dreamin', kid, is no way to go through life.

DONNY: Look, Charlie, that's all very interesting. But here's the thing. In my life from my . . . whatever. I don't know about the roads and the paths and all that. But I do know that I love her. I love her. I know she'll always be in my life. I want her to be happy. But I'm not in love with her.

CHARLIE: Do you beat off to her?

DONNY: Charlie, Charlie . . .

CHARLIE: What?

DONNY: Charlie, Charlie Brown! I love you, baby. But I ain't near stoned enough to talk about my masturbation habits with you.

CHARLIE: Don't be bashful.

DONNY: It's not that. It's just that . . .

CHARLIE: The sign of a truly confident man is a man who can admit to his own masturbation.

DONNY: I mean, I'm not saying I haven't tried it.

CHARLIE: You'll know if you're in love with the woman. The supreme test is the beat-off test. And believe you me, my dick has fooled me many times into thinking that absolute cunts were beautiful, well-rounded people. But I wasn't in love with the person. I was creating a person that lived inside this fucking fabulous body. You know, the supple breasts, tight stomach, skin so soft you don't want to stop caressing it. That shit blinds you into thinking that she's a cool woman. I don't particularly think that about Maggie. I mean, she's a beautiful woman, but in a down-to-earth well-rounded type of way.

DONNY: She's a great woman. She's gonna make some guy really happy someday. It's not gonna be me, but . . .

CHARLIE: Why not?

DONNY: Because what I've been . . .

CHARLIE: You can be that guy.

DONNY: But I'm not. I . . .

CHARLIE: Be that guy, Donny.

DONNY: I'm . . .

CHARLIE: Ah, ahhhhh, be that guy, Donny.

DONNY: OK.

CHARLIE: You're the guy.

DONNY: OK. I'm the guy. But the thing is . . .

CHARLIE: Stop it right now. And decide to be the man you've always secretly wanted to be.

(Donny is silent. Charlie gets up for a beer.)

CHARLIE: Did you know that Earl Johnson was a chronic masturbator?

DONNY: No I didn't.

CHARLIE: I mean constantly. Before games. After games. He used to do it in front of the other players. That always seemed a little strange to me. I mean, here's the other guys getting ready for the game and the best running back in the NFL is walking around the locker room with a hard-on.

DONNY: Charlie.

CHARLIE: Smaller than you might think too.

DONNY: Oh my God.

CHARLIE: Because he was a large black man.

DONNY: Yes he was.

CHARLIE: His thighs were immense.

DONNY: I can imagine.

CHARLIE: And here he was proudly walking around with this little pencil dick sticking out of these gigantic black thighs. It was a striking image.

DONNY: I bet.

DONNY: Oh, thank God they're back.

CHARLIE: Don't forget now. Watch for the subtleties.

DONNY: Right.

CHARLIE: I'm gonna teach you to be perceptive.

DONNY: I just hope they have the tequila.

SEA OF TRANQUILITY
Howard Korder

Dramatic
Ben and Johanssen, forties

> *Ben is a family counselor, living in Sante Fe. He has a dark secret*
> *in his past, and in this scene that past catches up with him. Ben's*
> *office. Ben, Johannsen leafing through a photography book.*

JOHANNSEN: You collect his work?

BEN: *(Of book.)* That was a gift.

JOHANNSEN: It's a tribute to the cowboy. A photographic tribute. Roping. Riding. Putting their boots on.

BEN: Mmm-hmm.

JOHANNSEN: Cowboys in the snow . . . chuck wagon. Actually some extremely luscious young ladies on motorcycles. He's got a studio in Dixon, now we saw in a gallery *here* one for eleven hundred, same print, directly from him, five hundred.

BEN: Well.

JOHANNSEN: Plus the drive, which is beautiful. Just beautiful up there. *(Pause.)*

BEN: Mister . . .

JOHANNSEN: Johannsen.

BEN: I'd love to go on chatting, I do have a client coming in.

JOHANNSEN: Are you sure?

BEN: Why wouldn't I be?

JOHANNSEN: Because I thought that might be something we'd talk about.

BEN: *We* would talk about.

JOHANNSEN: You and I. *(Pause.)*

BEN: Bohannon.

JOHANNSEN: Johannsen.

BEN: You called. Didn't you. You called my house.

JOHANNSEN: I spoke to your, son?

BEN: No, he's not my . . . *we* would talk about *my* client?

JOHANNSEN: Jennifer Newhall.

BEN: I don't know who — why would I discuss —

JOHANNSEN: Jennifer Astarte Newhall. Is a client. Patient. Whatever you like to call her. Of yours.

BEN: My client list is confidential.

JOHANNSEN: That's an ethical issue, is it?

BEN: Who are you, Mr. Johannsen?

JOHANNSEN: I represent the Sea Organization. Sea, like the ocean.

BEN: And that is —

JOHANNSEN: Affiliated with Religious Technologies Incorporated.

BEN: What is that?

JOHANNSEN: It's a corporation based in Los Angeles. *(Pause.)*

BEN: You're a Scientologist.

JOHANNSEN: I'm an attorney.

BEN: For the Scientologists.

JOHANNSEN: For the Sea Organization. And Ms. Newhall has asked me to intervene on her behalf.

BEN: What for? *(Pause.)* I'm sorry, did I say something funny? I asked what for.

JOHANNSEN: She wishes to let you know that she no longer requires your services. And she's authorized me to pay you in full for any fees incurred up to this point.

BEN: And she made this decision when?

JOHANNSEN: Sometime after your previous session.

BEN: I find that hard to believe.

JOHANNSEN: Well —

BEN: Because she seemed particularly eager to deal with her problems in counseling.

JOHANNSEN: That would make her a client, wouldn't it?

BEN: Whatever she *is,* she's looking for help.

JOHANNSEN: You must have been mistaken.

BEN: I don't think so.

JOHANNSEN: Really? You're never wrong? You're an infallible judge of human behavior?

BEN: I know when people need guidance. And Astarte — Jennifer —

JOHANNSEN: Has decided to seek that *guidance* somewhere else. I'm sure that's a blow to your ego, but that *is* the situation. *(Pause. Holding out a check.)* Cashier's check for one thousand dollars. I hope that's sufficient.

BEN: No.

JOHANNSEN: That's not enough?

BEN: It's too much.

JOHANNSEN: The check is cut. You might as well keep it. *(He places the check on the coffee table.)* And I would need copies of any records you have. Regarding your sessions.

BEN: Why?

JOHANNSEN: For whatever future course of treatment Ms. Newhall decides to pursue.

BEN: Her new therapist is free to contact me for that. Which is usually how it's done. *(Pause.)*

JOHANNSEN: I really am trying to make this easy for you.

BEN: What does that mean?

JOHANNSEN: That there is no pressing reason for any of what happened between you and Ms. Newhall to be made public.

BEN: *Between* us? Nothing happened,

JOHANNSEN: Dr. Green

BEN: She came in here for counseling

JOHANNSEN: You assaulted her.

BEN: What?

JOHANNSEN: We have a sworn affidavit

BEN: No no.

JOHANNSEN: During your session you forcibly and without her consent —

BEN: I would like to talk to, Jennifer personally —

JOHANNSEN: That's not possible.

BEN: Why? *(Pause.)* Where is she? I —

JOHANNSEN: She is safely —

BEN: Is she in California? You brought her there?

JOHANNSEN: I think the important issue —

BEN: You don't know where she is. Do you.

JOHANNSEN: Ms. Newhall has the right to come and go —

BEN: You're looking for her.

JOHANNSEN: — whenever and wherever —

BEN: Because of, what, this Donald person? Is that who you're after?

JOHANNSEN: You might want to concentrate on —

BEN: You bribe me. Threaten me —

JOHANNSEN: Whatever *your* perception —

BEN: Is this your *job?* What you *do?* Hunting down, do you call them, dissidents? Traitors? You think you're *helping* these people? *(Pause.)*

JOHANNSEN: What do you know about Jennifer?

BEN: Quite a bit.

JOHANNSEN: You didn't know her first name. I assume you don't know there's an outstanding warrant for her arrest in Los Angeles County.

BEN: What for?

JOHANNSEN: Vagrancy. Fraud. Violation of copyright. Possession of stolen goods. She and her *mentor* there had a nice little scam going. Claiming to be sanctioned of the church. Taking money from distressed people for help he had no authority to give. It came to well over twenty thousand dollars. She get around to mentioning that? *(Pause.)* There *is* an affidavit, Dr. Green. It *is* signed by Ms. Newhall. Obviously I'm not here to offer you advice. But you might want to consider what a charge like this could do to someone not very well established. In what is not a very large town.

BEN: Where is she? *(Pause.)* I would like to talk to her. For her sake. *(Pause.)* Do you care what happens to that girl at all?

JOHANNSEN: Did you care what happened to your client in Connecticut?

BEN: What client?

JOHANNSEN: The one you were screwing. The one who shot herself. In your car. On the Merritt Parkway. *(Pause.)* Quite a comedown, isn't it? From psychiatry to family counseling? I suppose you didn't have a choice. Since they threatened to take away your license. No one has to know that here. *Doctor.*

BEN: She — I *ended* it, and she was *suffering,* from —

JOHANNSEN: A chemical disorder? Still so much we don't understand? The deep enigma of human —

BEN: I was a different person then. If I could change it I would.

JOHANNSEN: But you can't. So what's that? "Wisdom"? *(Pause.)* You know,

I spent a lot of time in offices like this. Talked about my father. My feelings of alienation. My fear of commitment. It never solved anything. I found something that works. I want to protect it.

BEN: You came all the way from Los Angeles to tell me that?

JOHANNSEN: No. We time-share at Rancho Encantado. We love it for Christmas. *(He stands.)* We have a common cause, Dr. Green. We'd both like to do good for Ms. Newhall. *I'd* like to know what you discussed in this room. Let's concentrate on that.

BEN: Whatever she said — whatever you want me to think she said — you know it's not true.

JOHANNSEN: I don't know that at all. I do have a sense of what people are willing to believe. In the end that seems more important. *(He starts out, turns at the door.)* The check is on your table. *(He exits. Ben sits there. After a moment he takes out a pack of cigarettes. He lights one, takes a long drag, and slowly lets out the smoke.)*

SECOND
Neal Utterback

Dramatic
Davey, late twenties; Jake, early forties

> *Jake and Davey have been hired to kidnap a man they know al-
> most nothing about. For Davey, Jake is a kind of "big brother fig-
> ure." For Jake, this job may be his last chance for his and his son's
> future. Jake's the only one who knows who has hired them. The kid-
> napped man is in the room with them, tied to a chair. He either
> can't or won't talk. They are awaiting further instructions from their
> boss.*

DAVEY: *And.* In the, like 1500s — or maybe it was the fifteenth
    century — I can't remember — but these people were getting trashed,
    right? On like, mead, or nog, or whatever, and the alcohol was mix-
    ing with the lead in the — *(Davey makes a shape like a cup with his
    hands.)*

JAKE: Bucket?

DAVEY: No.

JAKE: Urn?

DAVEY: That they drank out of?

JAKE: A glass?

DAVEY: No, like a —

JAKE: A chalice?

DAVEY: Isn't that a chair?

JAKE: No, Davey, its not a chair.

DAVEY: I think it's a chair. A goblet. A lead goblet.

JAKE: Are you going to be like this all night? 'Cause I'll shoot you right
    now.

DAVEY: You wouldn't shoot me.

JAKE: Just finish your stupid story.

DAVEY: Where was I?

JAKE: They're drinking out of goblets.

DAVEY: And they're all passing out 'cause the alcohol is mixing with the lead so they look like they're dead and they buried them. Alive.

JAKE: Uh huh.

DAVEY: *Alive.*

JAKE: Yeah, I heard you.

DAVEY: And they didn't have enough coffins or whatever, so they dug these people back up and found scratch marks on the inside.

JAKE: Uh huh.

DAVEY: They were buried alive.

JAKE: Yes, I know.

DAVEY: So, they started attaching strings to people's fingers when they buried them and the strings were attached to a bell, which is where we get/

JAKE AND DAVEY: /Dead ringer.

JAKE: You're a wealth.

DAVEY: You know this?

JAKE: Everyone knows this.

DAVEY: I didn't know this.

JAKE: Everyone except you.

DAVEY: But I still don't know why "dead ringer" means something that looks just like something else. Buried alive, can you imagine? Scary, huh?

JAKE: What's *scary* is that the bulk of your knowledge comes from forwarded e-mails.

DAVEY: *(To Man.)* You were scared, weren't you?

(Man doesn't move.)

DAVEY: Did you know that some of the most famous deaths are fakes?

JAKE: What are you talking about?

DAVEY: Like JFK, the president. There's actually a group of people who believe JFK wasn't shot at all. It was his dippledonger and that the real/

JAKE: /Doppelgänger.

DAVEY: What?

JAKE: His doppelgänger.

DAVEY: What's that?

JAKE: What you're trying to say.

DAVEY: Dippledonger.

JAKE: No, doppelgänger.

DAVEY: I don't think that's right.

JAKE: His double?

DAVEY: Like his evil twin but maybe not evil.

JAKE: The word is doppelgänger.

DAVEY: Whatever, I'm not going to argue over Semitism.

JAKE: Semantics.

DAVEY: Why you gotta correct everything I say?

JAKE: Because everything you say is wrong.

DAVEY: Death freaks me out.

JAKE: Everybody dies.

DAVEY: Yeah, exactly. But you don't know how or when but you know it's gonna happen. Buried alive. I can't imagine a worse way to die.

JAKE: Would you just shut the hell up, *please?*

DAVEY: What? Are we just gonna sit here in silence?

JAKE: Yeah. *(Silence.)*

DAVEY: A rusty nail driven through your skull.

JAKE: What?

DAVEY: That's worse.

JAKE: Well, yeah, I guess so.

DAVEY: You sure you got a good signal?

JAKE: What?

DAVEY: On your phone?

JAKE: Yeah.

DAVEY: The storm may be interfering.

JAKE: I got a good signal.

DAVEY: Do you think he's gonna call?

JAKE: Yes.

DAVEY: I don't think I've ever been up in this neighborhood before.

JAKE: I had a girlfriend lived up here once.

DAVEY: Nice?

JAKE: Yeah, it's a nice neighborhood.

DAVEY: No, your girlfriend.

JAKE: What?

DAVEY: Was she nice?

JAKE: No, she was a bitch.

DAVEY: Oh. *(Silence.)*

DAVEY: Yeah, relationships are tough. *(Goes to the window.)* It's nice up here. I could live up here. Shitty apartment, though. You got a shitty apartment, dude. Man, look at the snow.

JAKE: Get away from the window.

DAVEY: It's really snowing.

JAKE: It's winter. That happens.

DAVEY: They're saying it's going to be the worst snowstorm ever.

JAKE: Well, they're idiots.

DAVEY: *(Singing.)* "Oh, come all ye faithful, joyful/"

JAKE: /Don't do that.

DAVEY: It's Christmas.

JAKE: *(Looks at his watch.)* Not yet.

DAVEY: *(Looking out the window.)* Man, it is really coming down.

JAKE: *(Being very clear.)* Get away from the window.

DAVEY: What if we get snowed in here for weeks with this guy? Dude, we'd have to eat each other.

JAKE: Why would we have to eat each other?

DAVEY: I bet this guy doesn't have any food in this place. *(To Man.)* You don't have anything to eat, do you? *(Goes to the kitchen.)* Dude, this creepy silent bastard doesn't have . . . Pop-Tarts, he has Pop-Tarts. And he's got —

JAKE: Why don't you go get something and bring it back?

DAVEY: I'm not goin' out there again.

JAKE: Then shut up.

DAVEY: . . . Would you eat me?

JAKE: Excuse me?

DAVEY: If we got snowed in here forever, would you eat me?

JAKE: I'm sure the neighbors have food.

DAVEY: Hypothetically, sayin' they don't. Would you eat me?

JAKE: Davey.

DAVEY: Yeah?

JAKE: I think I can say without reservation that I would never eat you.

DAVEY: That would be a pretty horrible way to die, huh?

JAKE: Sure.

DAVEY: . . . I'd eat you.

JAKE: Fine.

DAVEY: 'Cause I sure the hell ain't gonna starve to death. That'd really suck.
(Jake picks up his cell phone. He dials.)

DAVEY: Whataya doin', Jake?

JAKE: Checkin' messages. And don't use my name.

DAVEY: You called me Davey.

JAKE: No, I didn't.

DAVEY: Yeah, you did.

JAKE: No. I didn't.

DAVEY: *(To Man.)* He did, didn't he?

JAKE: Oh God, I'm in hell.

DAVEY: Did he call?

JAKE: . . . No.

DAVEY: I'm serious. It is really coming down. Come look.
(Jake doesn't.)

DAVEY: Damn, I hate the winter. I hate the cold. When I was living in
Florida, man . . . You ever been to Miami? It is paradise. Hotties walking around sh-boom titties all sh-bang. I had bitches smokin' my bong
every night, man. It was the goddamn Garden of Eden.

JAKE: So, why'd you come to New York?

DAVEY: Dude, Miami's expensive.
(Silence.)

DAVEY: . . . You hungry? You look hungry.

JAKE: No.

DAVEY: You want a Pop-Tart? *(To Man.)* Dude, can we have a Pop-Tart?

JAKE: We're not eating his food.

DAVEY: We could order something.

JAKE: Are you nuts?

DAVEY: I dunno.

JAKE: . . . I look hungry?

DAVEY: Yeah, you know?

JAKE: What does that mean?

DAVEY: It means you look hungry. What do you mean what does it mean?

JAKE: Am I not being clear?

DAVEY: I'm just asking.

JAKE: Because I want to be clear.

DAVEY: I know that.

JAKE: Do you?

DAVEY: Of course.

JAKE: Do you *know* that?

DAVEY: I know that.

JAKE: Good.

DAVEY: Of course, I know that.

JAKE: Because all I want from life — you hear me? — All I ever want, when they bury me, lay me dead in the ground, and tie a stupid string to *my* finger — you know what I want my grave to say?

DAVEY: I don't think they still tie string/

JAKE: /"He was clear." No bullshit, no confusion. Clear.

DAVEY: Yeah, dude, you're totally clear.

JAKE: That's all I want.

DAVEY: I can see through you, you're so clear.

JAKE: That's all I want.

(Silence.)

DAVEY: It's hard to know though, isn't it?

JAKE: What is?

DAVEY: Who we are or what we truly want.

JAKE: No, it's not. You just choose.

DAVEY: Do you ever wish you had a dippledonger?

JAKE: Doppelgänger.

DAVEY: Like . . . the one of you that's really you . . . the *you*-you . . . and the other one, the one who takes all of the risks, makes the mistakes.

JAKE: The you-*who*.

DAVEY: The one that makes all of the mistakes.

JAKE: What?

DAVEY: That's who.

JAKE: Who what?

DAVEY: The other you.

JAKE: Yeah, the you-*who*.

DAVEY: The one that makes all of the . . . did we just go into some parallel Abbott and Costello!

JAKE: /You said the *you*-you and I said the you-*who,* who is the other you . . . the you *who* could make . . .

DAVEY AND JAKE: All the mistakes.

JAKE: Get it?

DAVEY: Got it.

SECURITY
Israel Horovitz

Seriocomic
Zelly, thirties, White; Webster, thirties, Black

Zelly and Webster are security guards at an airport.

(Stage lights up suddenly on Zelly and Webster, mid-sentence. Both are thirtyish. Zelly is White, Webster is Black. They wear black pants, white shirts, black neckties. Both wear pager-phones on their belts. We shouldn't realize that they're security guards until later in the scene, when they redress, strapping on guns/holsters, putting on uniform jackets. They are, at the moment, on a lunch break, eating sandwiches, drinking soda from cans. From time to time, Webster reads a newspaper.)

ZELLY: You see what I'm sayin'? She couldn't if she would.

WEBSTER: That makes no sense. If she would, she would. If she couldn't, she couldn't.

ZELLY: You still see my point, though, don't'cha?

WEBSTER: I don't.

ZELLY: Whatever. *(Webster shrugs, which angers Zelly.)* I'm saying that she would meet up with me, in a *heartbeat,* but the husband would find out and kill her, 'cause he follows her everywhere. He's, like, *tuned in* to her. Got her wired with a beeper — she's got to check in by cell phone, every fifteen minutes. Man's got computer chips in her fuckin' *socks!* So, even if she would, she couldn't. Now, you see what I'm sayin'?

WEBSTER: *(Makes "time-out" signal with his hands.)* Time.

ZELLY: What?

WEBSTER: You're missing some major info, Z.

ZELLY: What?

WEBSTER: They're split up.

ZELLY: What are you tellin' me?

WEBSTER: They're split up. The husband's living in some weird place. An 'M' state. Montana . . . Maine . . . Michigan. . . . Shelly's been seein' Ronnie What'sis from Accounting for maybe two three weeks.

ZELLY: Bullshit.

WEBSTER: Serious.

ZELLY: Bullshit.

WEBSTER: I'm talkin' hugging in public, quick kisses. . . .

ZELLY: Bullshit.

WEBSTER: . . . Hands and shit.

ZELLY: You are fucking with me.

WEBSTER: Not. I see them on this train, her hand's on his leg, way *here. (Webster touches his own thigh, just below the crotch.)* Friendship is in her hand, like, maybe *here . . . (His hand on his own knee.)* Let's say maybe knee to maybe mid-thigh. I am seein' tree-line to dick! This is not friendship.

ZELLY: You're fuckin' with me, Webster.

WEBSTER: On my mother's grave! *(Suddenly.)* Massachusetts! *(Explains.)* The husband.

ZELLY: Why am I just now hearing this?!

WEBSTER: She calls him "big guy"?

ZELLY: What's this?

WEBSTER: I know. I'm goin' to myself, if she's callin' this runty little dude "big guy," he's gotta' be blowin' his paycheck on Internet *Viagra.*

ZELLY: Ronnie. the flabby little Jew from Accounting'?

WEBSTER: Fogliato.

ZELLY: Him. Ronnie *Fag*lialo.

WEBSTER: Ronnie Fogliato.

ZELLY: Him.

WEBSTER: I think he's Italian.

ZELLY: That' a Jew, if I ever saw one.

WEBSTER: She's a Jew.

(Webster picks up copy of New York Post, *begins to read. After a moment . . .)*

ZELLY: Why are you fuckin' with me?

WEBSTER: She's a Jew, man. Shelly fuckin' Goldfarb. That's a definite Jew name.

ZELLY: Webster, will you get fuckin' real! She's a *redhead!*

WEBSTER: Shelly *Goldfarb!*

ZELLY: Bruce *Springsteen!*

WEBSTER: Shelly *Goldfarb!*

ZELLY: Lenny *Kravitz!*

WEBSTER: I'm sayin' "save your breath to cool your oatmeal," Z. I'm tellin'
you, man: Shelly Goldfarb is surfin' a whole 'nother wave.

ZELLY: Bitch is givin' me looks, no more than two days ago.

WEBSTER: You know what they say: "once the floodgates open . . . "

ZELLY: What? Once the floodgates open, what?

(Webster looks up from his newspaper, stymied.)

WEBSTER: Who the fuck knows? Flooding.

ZELLY: What are you givin' me, you?

WEBSTER: You see this?

ZELLY: What?

WEBSTER: Now, they're sayin' Osama Bin Laden is definitely alive.

ZELLY: I saw this on TV.

WEBSTER: One day, he's dead, the next day, he's alive.

ZELLY: He's alive. He's makin' videos. He ain't doing that dead. *(Beat.)*
Fuckin' world's a mess. You see the new suicide bomber slut on TV,
this morning?

WEBSTER: My cable's shut off.

ZELLY: What'? She didn't pay your bill, again?

WEBSTER: Don't get me started.

ZELLY: School bus full'a little kids. *(Makes sound of bomb exploding.)*
PCOOOWWWW!

WEBSTER: World's goin' nuts.

ZELLY: You ain't got kids.

WEBSTER: I got kids.

ZELLY: Livin' with you.

WEBSTER: Yuh, so?

ZELLY: You put your kids on a school bus, every morning, you see shit
like that on TV, gets you crazy. Kid gets on his bus, the bus driver
blows up. What *is* that shit?

WEBSTER: Thank God it ain't happenin' here.

ZELLY: Give it five minutes. That's what Bin Laden's sayin' on his new video. Fuckin' Arabs love him. He's livin' high, somewhere, you can bet on that — probably in Saudi-land. Man hides in a filthy cave for three years, pops up in a video wearing a spandy-clean white dress? I don't think so! Probably sharin' a duplex with Saddam in Syria.

WEBSTER: *(Reads aloud from his newspaper.)* "The Roman Catholic Archdiocese of Boston is likely to declare bankruptcy as a way to grapple with the lawsuits filed as part of the sex abuse crisis."

ZELLY: I saw this on TV.

(Small pause, And then . . .)

WEBSTER: You're Catholic, aren't you?

ZELLY: So what?

WEBSTER: You ever have any of that shit happen?

ZELLY: Not in Bayonne, New Jersey. Priest ever tries that shit, he ends up in a barrel. *(Beat.)* Assistant scoutmaster once tried something with my cousin Raymond.

WEBSTER: Catholic?

ZELLY: My cousin?

WEBSTER: Scoutmaster.

ZELLY: Assistant Scoutmaster. Who the fuck knows what he was. It was Scouts! Nondenominational. Could've been anything. Big German guy, blonde, ripped — worked out with weights. Carl. . . . Something German. *(And then . . .)* He put his finger in Raymond's mouth.

WEBSTER: You are making this up!

ZELLY: So help me, God!

WEBSTER: In his mouth.

ZELLY: In his mouth,

WEBSTER: How'd he do that?

ZELLY: I dunno. We were on a camping trip up in the Watchung Reservation . . . in Jersey. He calls Raymond into his tent. Next thing I know, Raymond comes back, tells me.

WEBSTER: What did Raymond do'?

ZELLY: He bit the motherfucker! Damn near took off his finger!

WEBSTER: That's what I was thinkin'!

ZELLY: We were just kids. Raymond was scared he was gonna' get into trouble.

WEBSTER: That's the thing.

ZELLY: World's fucked up, isn't it?

WEBSTER: *(Referring to photo in his newspaper.)* You like Bush?

ZELLY: I dunno. I guess. He's tough.

WEBSTER: How so?

ZELLY: He ain't takin' any shit from anybody. He's standin' up to them.

WEBSTER: Him, personally, or him, sendin' other people's kids?

ZELLY: You don't like Bush?

WEBSTER: I don't.

ZELLY: Did you like Al Gore?

WEBSTER: The man put me to sleep. He would speak, I would nod. Good thing he quit. If the Democrats ran him, again, he might have *actually* lost.

ZELLY: Who do you want for President?

(Beat.)

WEBSTER: Denzel Washington.

ZELLY: You're fuckin' with me.

WEBSTER: Denzel would be cool.

ZELLY: He's an actor.

WEBSTER: And Bush ain't? Denzel could pull things together, a shitload easier than Bush. Denzel goes on TV, says "Hey, Osama Bin Laden, come on out and let's talk!" Bin Laden's comes right the fuck out'ta his cave, man, goin' "Yo! This shit is *cool!* I'm gonna' meet Denzel Washington!" Let's face it, Z. *Everybody* wants to meet Denzel Washington!

ZELLY: World's a mess, man!

WEBSTER: Can't blame Denzel!

ZELLY: What the fuck kinda' name is Denzel?

WEBSTER: Black name. It's a racial thing. When you're black, you gotta' give your kid a black name, otherwise, nobody would ever know he was black. You see what I'm sayin', Zelly?

ZELLY: Somebody must've dropped you on your head, when you were little, man. You are *cracked.*

(Beat.)

WEBSTER: What kind of name is Zelly?

ZELLY: Nickname.

WEBSTER: What's your real name?

ZELLY: Zelly's short for my real name.

WEBSTER: What's your real name?

ZELLY: I don't use it.

WEBSTER: Yuh, but what is it?

(Beat.)

ZELLY: Zelmo.

WEBSTER: You shittin' me?

ZELLY: I never use it.

WEBSTER: What the fuck kind of name is Zelmo?

ZELLY: It's a *white* name, asshole!

WEBSTER: No. Hold! I know a couple of while folk, and none of them ain't named no fuckin' Zelmo!

ZELLY: It's a family name, from back in Europe.

WEBSTER: You from Europe?

ZELLY: You know I'm not from fuckin' Europe!

WEBSTER: Where you from?

ZELLY: Bayonne. You fuckin' know this.

WEBSTER: You got a lot of dudes livin' in Bayonne named Zelmo?

ZELLY: Fuck you, Webster! You're really startin' to annoy me! *(And then . . .)* Where'd your mother come up with "Webster"? Off the cover of the fuckin' dictionary? What? She was too lazy to even open the thing up and look *inside?*

WEBSTER: Fuck you, Zelmo!

Scenes for Two Women

EVERYTHING WILL BE DIFFERENT

Mark Schultz

Seriocomic
Charlotte and Heather, teenagers

> *Charlotte is an increasingly disturbed girl whose mother has recently passed away. Here, her best friend Heather is visiting her in her room at home. We don't know it in this scene (we only find out much later in the play), but Heather is a figment of Charlotte's imagination. The lights in this scene should be soft, beautiful — almost magical. Charlotte's room.*

CHARLOTTE: He's like obsessed.

HEATHER: He is.

CHARLOTTE: He's like really obsessed. I can't go.

HEATHER: You can't go?

CHARLOTTE: I can't go. Wherever.

HEATHER: So like he locks the door? Like he won't let you out?

CHARLOTTE: He yelled at me and he tore up my luggage.

HEATHER: What?

CHARLOTTE: He yelled at me and he tore up my luggage. He called me ugly.

HEATHER: Your dad?

CHARLOTTE: Yes.

HEATHER: You're just a little challenged is all.

CHARLOTTE: I am not ugly.

HEATHER: You are not ugly.

CHARLOTTE: I know. I want him to die. Do I have acne?

HEATHER: I don't even know what that is.

CHARLOTTE: Acne?

HEATHER: No. You don't. Wait. Yeah.

CHARLOTTE: Yes?

HEATHER: Yes.

CHARLOTTE: God. I want him to die.

HEATHER: He lets you out for school, right?

CHARLOTTE: Maybe. I don't know. It's the weekend. And I'm like grounded forever.

HEATHER: He has to let you go to school.

CHARLOTTE: I don't know. I can't do anything.

HEATHER: He has to let you go to school. That's like, illegal if he doesn't. It's so illegal.

CHARLOTTE: I know. Is every dad like this? Is your dad like this?

HEATHER: No. Like he's weird and all? But he lets me drive? And I don't have a license or anything. And sometimes like I'm all: Can I borrow your credit card? And he's like: Why? And I'm all: So I can buy some clothes? And he's like: Sure. And I totally use his credit card. I love him.

CHARLOTTE: That's like perfect.

HEATHER: He listens to Neil Diamond. That is not perfect.

CHARLOTTE: I like Neil Diamond.

HEATHER: No one likes Neil Diamond.

CHARLOTTE: I guess you're right.

HEATHER: I know I'm right.

CHARLOTTE: Heather? What would I do without you?

HEATHER: I don't know. Rot?

CHARLOTTE: Probably. *(Beat.)* I always wanted my name to be Caroline. Like Sweet Caroline.

HEATHER: There are so many better things to want.

CHARLOTTE: I guess.

HEATHER: Trust me. There are.

CHARLOTTE: Like what?

HEATHER: Like love. And fame. And a *nice* outfit. And a massage. And power. And power. And love. And love. And love. Also love.

CHARLOTTE: If I ever get out of here.

HEATHER: You'll get out.

CHARLOTTE: I will be so loved.

HEATHER: You will be.

CHARLOTTE: Everyone will want me.

HEATHER: I want you.

CHARLOTTE: Do you?

(Beat.)

HEATHER: You know what you need? You need to like do something for you. Like go to a spa or something. You so deserve it. We should go. My dad'll pay.

CHARLOTTE: You're such a good friend.

HEATHER: I know.

CHARLOTTE: I love you Heather. (Beat.) We can do anything, can't we? Like everyone says You can do anything. But that really means something with us, doesn't it?

HEATHER: It does.

CHARLOTTE: It so does.

(Beat.)

HEATHER: Hey I'm really sorry about your mom.

CHARLOTTE: I know.

HEATHER: It's just so sad.

CHARLOTTE: I know.

HEATHER: Are you sad?

CHARLOTTE: Yeah.

HEATHER: Me too. She was so pretty. She was like, the best mom.

CHARLOTTE: I know.

HEATHER: With like the cupcakes? And the chicken pot pie? Oh my God, I loved your mother's chicken pot pie. It was like. Not even chicken. But. More than chicken. Or something. I don't know. It was just really good. I wish she was my mom.

CHARLOTTE: I know.

HEATHER: I wish my mom would die? Cause she's worthless? And that somehow, like in the next world or the afterlife or whatever, she would meet your mom, and like, send her back.

CHARLOTTE: Me too.

HEATHER: But it always happens to the beautiful ones Charlotte.

CHARLOTTE: What?

HEATHER: Early death.

CHARLOTTE: Really?

HEATHER: Of course. Everything beautiful dies. Only the ugly things stick
    around. That's why, if I live past thirty-five? I will be so upset.
CHARLOTTE: That is such a good point.
HEATHER: I know.

(Beat. Heather stares at Charlotte.)

CHARLOTTE: What?
HEATHER: Nothing. Just. Sometimes when I look at you? I can see her.
    This beautiful thing. Sort of hiding. And lost. In you.
CHARLOTTE: Really?
HEATHER: You just need to let it out is all.
CHARLOTTE: Really?
HEATHER: Definitely. We just need to focus.
CHARLOTTE: Oh my God. I will. I so will.
HEATHER: Good.
CHARLOTTE: You're the best, Heather.
HEATHER: I know. *(Beat.)* Hey Charlotte? I gotta go, OK. I have a date.
    With a really hot guy. And I gotta go.
CHARLOTTE: You're so lucky.
HEATHER: I know.
CHARLOTTE: He's cute?
HEATHER: Of course.
CHARLOTTE: You're so lucky.
HEATHER: I know. He has a brother. They're twins.
CHARLOTTE: You're so lucky.
HEATHER: I know. I gotta go.
CHARLOTTE: OK. Go.
HEATHER: Gone.
CHARLOTTE: Bye.
        Bye.
        Good-bye.

EVERYTHING WILL BE DIFFERENT

Mark Schultz

Dramatic
Charlotte and Heather, teens

> *Charlotte has recently lost her mother, and she is a very disturbed
> girl, living more and more in a fantasy world, which she discusses
> with her best friend, Heather who, we realize just after this scene,
> exists only in Charlotte's imagination.*

(Soft, gentle light. Again, something beautiful.)

HEATHER: So is it true? Oh my God is it? Wow. That is such a coup. That
  is such a big coup. You're like, I don't know. You're my hero. That's
  awesome. I'm totally jealous.

CHARLOTTE: He's so cute.

HEATHER: Hot.

CHARLOTTE: Hot.

HEATHER: He is hot. Oh my God. Do you love him?

CHARLOTTE: I think so.

HEATHER: Why?

CHARLOTTE: I don't know.

HEATHER: You don't have to.

CHARLOTTE: I know.

HEATHER: Wait on love. OK? That comes later. I know what I'm talking
  about. You'll only hurt yourself.

CHARLOTTE: OK.

HEATHER: Trust me.

CHARLOTTE: OK.

HEATHER: Did you suck his dick?

CHARLOTTE: No.

HEATHER: Good. It is so overrated.

CHARLOTTE: We just started going out.

HEATHER: Whatever. Look at you all shy. There is no need to be shy. OK. When he starts to love you like a lot? He'll totally want you to suck his dick. And that's normal and everything? But make him wait. It is no fun.

CHARLOTTE: OK.

HEATHER: I know what I'm talking about.

CHARLOTTE: You're the best.

HEATHER: I know. You've seen him naked?

CHARLOTTE: Heather . . .

HEATHER: That is a totally valid question. Don't Heather me. You sound like my dad. You should really see him naked. Not my dad. Your guy. Size him up. Make sure he's like. OK. And not. Retarded or whatever.

CHARLOTTE: He's not retarded.

HEATHER: Whatever. You need to know. This is important. Has he kissed you?

CHARLOTTE: Not yet.

HEATHER: Are you really going out with him?

CHARLOTTE: Heather. Yes.

HEATHER: 'Cause it sounds like he's your brother or something. I mean, what have you done? Have you done anything? Have you like gone out or whatever? Have you held hands? I mean, Charlotte. Going out does not mean like repartee. You know. Or whatever. Dating is not a conversation.

CHARLOTTE: I know. We're going slow.

HEATHER: Going slow? You could not be going slower. Charlotte. Take control. Bull by the horns. Hand jobs are fine at this stage. And fucking's OK too I guess. But draw the line at blow jobs. I am so serious.

CHARLOTTE: I will.

HEATHER: Not until you're ready. You'll just hurt yourself. Anyway it takes time to develop good blowing skills. Maybe you should practice. Like find someone to practice on?

CHARLOTTE: Like cheat on him?

HEATHER: It is not cheating. OK. It is practice. It's like when you practice anything. You're not cheating the final whatever. Performance. Or audience. Or. Whatever. It is just not cheating.

CHARLOTTE: OK.

HEATHER: The world is not so cut and dry, Charlotte. This or that. There is so much in between.

CHARLOTTE: I know.

HEATHER: So act like it. OK?

CHARLOTTE: I will.

HEATHER: Don't just say it.

CHARLOTTE: OK.

HEATHER: No one is going to wait for you to be what you are. OK? And no one is going to care about you if you *aren't* what you *are.* So you have to be gorgeous *now,* Charlotte. Or you never will be. Your eyes look really nice today.

CHARLOTTE: Thanks. That is so profound. About the being and stuff.

HEATHER: I know. I'm like the Dalai Lama or whatever. But without like all the bad clothes and the shaved head and the Third World country.

CHARLOTTE: You're like my sister, Heather.

HEATHER: Isn't it fun?

CHARLOTTE: I want so much for us.

HEATHER: I know. Me too. Oh my God. I almost forgot. I brought you something from Mexico?

CHARLOTTE: What is it?

HEATHER: It's a peso. Which means you can't really do anything with it? But it's from another country. And I thought of you.

CHARLOTTE: It's beautiful.

HEATHER: I know. Isn't it pretty? With the bird?

CHARLOTTE: Yes.

HEATHER: I thought of you. How you couldn't come. Cause of your dad?

CHARLOTTE: I know. He's horrible.

HEATHER: The beaches are so pretty. And everyone is so friendly. They're all like full of love or whatever. And they'll do anything for a dollar. Or even a peso. But I saved that one for you. I was gonna buy a monkey with it? Or a cucumber? Or a boy? But my daddy wouldn't let me. So I saved it for you.

CHARLOTTE: Thank you.

HEATHER: You should let me do your hair. You are so pretty, Charlotte. I'm so jealous.

CHARLOTTE: Why? You have the great dad. And the house. And the car. And the credit card. And Mexico.

HEATHER: I know. But you're so pretty. And lucky. With your boy. I don't have anybody right now.

CHARLOTTE: What about the twins?

HEATHER: Don't get me started on the twins.

CHARLOTTE: You have me.

HEATHER: *He* has you.

CHARLOTTE: I don't belong to him, Heather. I'm not his.

HEATHER: Promise me.

CHARLOTTE: Promise what?

HEATHER: That you're not his.

CHARLOTTE: I promise.

(*Beat.*)

HEATHER: Can I kiss you?

CHARLOTTE: What?

HEATHER: We should totally have like a lesbian moment right now.

CHARLOTTE: Heather?

HEATHER: What? (*Beat.*) It was joke. (*Beat.*) We should move to Mexico. Everyone is free in Mexico. You can do what you want. And the weather's nice. And there are pyramids. And jungles. And scorpions. And parrots? No one cares what you do. Everyone's a criminal anyway. It's where real life is. And real love. And we could live there. Together. Just us.

(*Slowly, awkwardly, they move to kiss each other.*)

HEATHER: Can I? (*Beat.*) I think your acne cleared up. That's so cute. Do you use the product now?

CHARLOTTE: Yes.

(*They kiss.*)

CHARLOTTE: I'm so. Happy. With you. Heather.

HEATHER: Me too.

(*They kiss.*)

CHARLOTTE: I think I'm gonna vomit.

HEATHER: It's OK. Just means you're excited. It's good.

(They kiss.)

CHARLOTTE: I gotta pee.

HEATHER: Hold it.

CHARLOTTE: I can't.

HARRY'S VOICE: *(Offstage.)* Charlotte?

HEATHER: Then don't.

(They kiss.)

HARRY'S VOICE: Who're you talking to?

HEATHER: I love you.

INTIMATE APPAREL
Lynn Nottage

Dramatic
Esther and Mayme, thirties, Black

> *Esther is a Black seamstress in New York in 1905. She lives in a*
> *boarding house for women. Mayme is a customer.*

> *(Another bedroom. A canopy bed dominates. Mayme, a strikingly beau-*
> *tiful African-American woman (thirty) sits at an upright piano. She plays*
> *a frenzied upbeat rag. Her silk robe is torn, and her face trembles with*
> *outrage. Esther bangs on the door, then finally enters carrying a carpet-*
> *bag.)*

ESTHER: I been knocking for ages. Didn't you hear me? . . . What's going
on? *(A moment.)*

MAYME: They really do make me sick. Always stinking of booze. And look
what he done. It's the only pretty thing I own and look what he done.
(Mayme pulls her torn silk robe tight around her body.)

ESTHER: That ain't nothing, I can fix it for you.

MAYME: All the pawing and pulling. For a dollar they think they own you.
(Mayme quickly washes her face and privates in a basin.) You don't ap-
prove of me, Esther. I don't mind. Sit. I'm awfully glad to see ya,
'am. When you knocked on the door, I thought Christ almighty, not
another one. I'm so damn tired, I don't know what to do.
(Mayme sits down at the upright piano and gracefully plays a slow well-
considered rag.)

ESTHER: Oh, pretty. Did you write that, Mayme?

MAYME: Yeah . . . *(Continuing to play.)* My daddy gave me twelve lashes
with a switch for playing this piece in our parlor. One for each year
I studied the piano. He was too proper to like anything colored, and
a syncopated beat was about the worst crime you could commit in
his household. *(Mayme stops playing.)* I woke up with the sudden urge
to play it.

ESTHER: You must have gotten a lot of licks in your time.

MAYME: Yeah, baby, I wasn't born this black and blue. *(Mayme picks up a bottle of moonshine and takes a belt.)*

ESTHER: That there the reason you tired, that ignorant oil is unforgiving. Best let it lie.

MAYME: Oh bother, stop playing mother hen and come show me what you got.

ESTHER: Anything else, Mistress?

MAYME: Hush your mouth, you're far too sweet for sarcasm. *(Esther pulls a corset from her bag. It's pale blue with lines of royal blue glass beads ornamenting the bodice, like Mrs. Van Buren's. Touched:)* Is that for me? *(Mayme leaps up from the piano and holds the corset up to her body.)*

ESTHER: I made one just like it for a lady on Fifth Avenue.

MAYME: It's so pretty. This is really for me? No kidding? Can I try it on?

ESTHER: Of course you can.

MAYME: Feel it. It feels like Fifth Avenue, does. You outdone yourself this time, honey.

ESTHER: Stop talking and put it on. *(Mayme gives Esther a kiss on the cheek.)* And look at the flowers, ain't they sweet? It took me a whole day just to sew them on. *(Mayme takes off her robe and puts on the corset.)*

MAYME: For shame. This the prettiest thing anybody ever made for me. Truly.

ESTHER: You know that white lady I talk about sometime, hold on . . . *(Mayme grabs the bedpost, as Esther pulls the corset tight.)* She keep asking me what they be wearing up in the tenderloin. All that money and high breeding and she want what you wearing.

MAYME: No kidding?

ESTHER: What she got, you want, what you got, she want.

MAYME: Onliest, I ain't got the money to pay for it. *(Mayme models the corset.)* Whatcha think? Do I look like a Fifth Avenue bird?

ESTHER: Grand. You look grand. Mr. Marks say, that satin foulard was made for the finest ladies in Paris.

MAYME: No kidding.

ESTHER: I wasn't going to buy it. But, oh Lord, if he didn't talk me into it.

MAYME: Mr. Marks? *(A moment.)* Who is this Mr. Marks?

ESTHER: He just a salesman. That's all.

MAYME: It sound to me like you bit sweet on him.

ESTHER: Me? Oh no, he a Jew.

(Mayme looks into Esther's eyes.)

MAYME: And? I been with a Jew, with a Turk even. And let me tell ya, a gentle touch is gold in any country.

ESTHER: I see the bodice is bit snug —

MAYME: Is he handsome?

ESTHER: I ain't noticed.

MAYME: Good patient, Esther. Come, he wouldn't be your first, would he?

ESTHER: I ain't listenin'.

MAYME: (Softening her tone.) You dear thing. (Mayme laughs long and hard. Esther doesn't respond.) No kidding. I can't even remember what it was like. Ain't that something.

ESTHER: Let's not talk about this.

MAYME: Mercy, what you must think of me. (Mayme, suddenly self-conscious, touches the beading on the corset.)

ESTHER: And if you must know, I'm being courted by a gentleman.

MAYME: Courted by a gentleman. Beg my pardon. Not that Panama man? Oh come on, don't tell me you still writing him.

ESTHER: He writing me.

MAYME: You'd rather a man all the way across the ocean then down Broadway. Are you expecting him to arrive in the mail like some tonic from a catalogue?

ESTHER: Please don't make sport, Mayme.

MAYME: I'm just playing with you.

ESTHER: (Wounded.) I ain't expectin' nothing. (A moment. Mayme acknowledges Esther's hurt. She caresses her friend's face.)

MAYME: Sure you are. Sure you are, honey. Who ain't? (Mayme sits on bed, beside Esther.) I am a concert pianist playing recitals for audiences in Prague and I have my own means, not bad for a colored girl from Memphis . . . (Mayme plays a few bars of classical music, perhaps allowing it to become a rag.) And Madame always takes tea twice a week with her dear friend Miss Esther Mills, who's known in circles for . . .

for what? I forget. *(Esther is reluctant to share her dream.)* Come on, Miss Esther, don't be proud.

ESTHER: I own a quaint beauty parlor for colored ladies.

MAYME: Of course.

ESTHER: The smart set. Someplace east of Amsterdam, fancy, where you get pampered and treated real nice. 'Cause no one does it for us. We just as soon wash our heads in a bucket and be treated like mules. But what I'm talking about is someplace elegant.

MAYME: Go on, missie, you too fancy for me.

ESTHER: When you come in Miss Mayme, I'll take your coat and ask, "Would you like a cup of tea?"

MAYME: Why, thank you.

ESTHER: And I'll open a book of illustrations, and show you the latest styles.

MAYME: I can pick anything in the book?

ESTHER: Yes.

MAYME: How about if I let you choose?

ESTHER: Very well. Make yourself comfortable, put your feet up, I know they're tired.

MAYME: Shucks, you don't know the half of it.

ESTHER: And in no time flat for the cost a ride uptown and back, you got a whole new look.

MAYME: Just like that? I reckon I'd pay someone good money to be treated like a lady. It would be worth two, three days on my back. Yes, it would.

ESTHER: You think so?

MAYME: I know so.

ESTHER: And if I told you I got a little something saved? I keep it sewed up in the lining of a crazy quilt.

MAYME: On a cold lonely night wouldn't that quilt be a poor woman's dream.

ESTHER: I been saving it slowly since I come North. It for that beauty parlor. I ain't told nobody that. Honest, for true.

MAYME: Where'd you get such a damn serious face?

ESTHER: Why not?

MAYME: Because, we just fooling that's all. I ain't been to Prague, ain't never gonna go to Prague.

ESTHER: But come, is this what you want to be doing ten years from now, twenty?

MAYME: You think I ain't tried to make a go of it. You think I just laid down and opened my legs 'cause it was easy. It don't look like nothing, but this saloon is better then a lot of them places, ask anybody. Only last night one of Bert Williams' musicians sat up front, and he stayed through the entire show. You think some of those gals in the big revues didn't start right where I am.

ESTHER: You got this beautiful piano that you play better than anyone I know. There are a dozen church choirs —

MAYME: Let me tell you, so many wonderful ideas been conjured in this room. They just get left right in that bed there, or on this piano bench. They are scattered all over this room. Esther, I ain't waiting for anybody to rescue me. My Panama man come and gone long time now. It sweet that he write you but, my dear, it ain't real.

ESTHER: Yes, he here in my pocket in a cambric walking suit, he has a heliotrope handkerchief stuffed in his pocket and a sweet way about him. He so far away, I can carry him in my pocket like a feather. *(Esther laughs and produces a letter from her apron.)*

MAYME: You're funny. You and your silly letter.

ESTHER: Ain't a week go by without one. It got so I know the postman by name. *(Esther holds out the letter.)*

MAYME: I ain't interested. Put it away.

ESTHER: C'mon Miss Mayme . . . don't be proud, you know you want to read it. *(Esther dangles the letter; threatening to put it away at any moment.)*

MAYME: Hell, give it here. *(Mayme snatches the letter and quickly peruses it. allowing herself a smile.)* Ooo.

ESTHER: What it say?

MAYME: Your man got himself a new pair of socks. Wait . . . uhoh, he askin' what you look like. Ain't you told him?

ESTHER: No. I'm afraid, I ain't known what to say.

MAYME: Tell him the truth.

ESTHER: That I don't look like much.

MAYME: You tell him that you're about as lovely a person as there is.

ESTHER: You know that ain't so.

MAYME: Of course, it is. And what does it matter? You think half the men that come in here bother looking at my face. No ma'am. He don't care about this. *(Mayme grabs Esther's face and gives her a kiss on the forehead. She playfully shows off her physical attributes which are accentuated by the formfitting lingerie.)* He interested in this, my dear. This is what he's asking about. *(Mayme laughs.)*

ESTHER: I wouldn't dare write about something like that. He Christian!

MAYME: And it's in his weakness that he'll find his strength. Hallelujah! C'mon, I'm just playing with you.

ESTHER: I'm being serious and you got your mind in the gutter.

MAYME: Oh for God's sake, the man just asking what you look like 'cause he want something pretty to think about come sundown.

ESTHER: You reckon? Then will you help me write something? *(Mayme hands back the letter to Esther.)*

MAYME: No, what about your white lady? Why not have her do it? *(A moment. Esther opens her carpetbag.)*

ESTHER: 'Cause I'm asking you, my friend.

MAYME: No, my writing ain't perfect.

ESTHER: Don't bother about the handwriting, we'll tell him I pricked my finger while sewing. He'll understand. Please.

MAYME: Oh. *(Mayme fetches a sheet of paper and a pen and sits on the bed. Esther sits next to her.)* I ain't romantic, I find this silly, really I do. Only 'cause it's you. So, how do I begin?

ESTHER: "Dear George." *(Mayme concentrates, then slowly writes.)*

MAYME: *(Savoring the notion.)* A love letter to a gentleman. Yes, I know. "Dear George, I write you wearing a lavender silk robe with —" *(Esther giggles.)*

THE LEFT HAND SINGING
Barbara Lebow

Honey and Linda, twenty

Honey and Linda are two college students who have vanished without a trace in the Deep South during Freedom Summer, 1964. Before this tragedy occurs, we meet them here in their dorm room.

(A small college, upstate, New York, late May 1964, around 10:15 P.M.. A women's dormitory room. There are muted posters featuring JFK, MLK Jr., Che, The Beatles. A football jersey reading "BUBBA," pink cheer-leading pom-poms and other bits of memorabilia adorn the walls. The two beds (one unmade), desks, floor pillows and spool table hold assorted books, clothing, LP albums from library, food.

A piece of piano music written for the left hand, such as "Ravel's Concerto for the Left Hand," is heard. As lights rise, the music lowers and shifts to a small phonograph. Linda and Honey are barefoot, in the midst of books, papers, notes, shoes, LPs. They are each reading and making notes. During these scenes, the students sit on floor, beds and, sometimes, chairs. The door is ajar.

Linda yawns, plays with her pencil, eats a potato chip, finishes a Coke. Finally, with a show of exhaustion, she falls on the unmade bed, putting her open book over her face.)

HONEY: *(Amused familiarity.)* What are you doing now?

LINDA: *(Lifting book bottom.)* I'm listening.

HONEY: No, you're not. Any second, you're going to start that awful snoring again.

LINDA: I told you, I never snore!

HONEY: You snore like a horse. With adenoids! Mouth all open and drooling.

LINDA: Liar!

HONEY: It kept me up half the night! Now you're gonna keep me from studying.

LINDA: It just so happens, I'm wide awake. Memorizing the music.

HONEY: And the Nietzsche by osmosis, I suppose. A brilliant way to study! Ravel, accompanied by — *(Snores loudly.)*

LINDA: All right, already! *(She slams the book onto the floor. Honey answers with a loud chair adjustment, Linda stomps her foot as she stands. She moves to the book and begins repeated rises on it. Pleased, in exercise rhythm.)* Osmosis by *foot* . . . of Nietzsche . . . And if Professor Dahlberg . . . plays the Ravel . . . for the exam . . . I'll remember it . . . Plus build my muscles.

HONEY: So you can chase after Wes on one of his endless hikes.

LINDA: So I can wear shorts.

HONEY: Nothing you do is gonna put any shape in those legs.

LINDA: Thanks a lot, pal!

HONEY: Heck! You're not going to study! You aim to slide past like always. Maybe you can afford that, but us po' scholarships can't get by with no Cs. *(She lifts the arm off the record.)*

LINDA: *(Stopping the rises.)* I never got a C in my life! Besides, whatever you accomplish here is nothing compared to what we're gonna be doing in Mississippi.

HONEY: *(After a beat.)* There's something I better tell you. You might not like this, but — *(Pause.)* I got a letter today. Curtis wants me to help him sell cars all summer instead.

LINDA: You're kidding!

HONEY: What's wrong with that? With him down at Morehouse and me up here the rest of the year. We both need the money. If he's going to law school and I'm gonna teach —

LINDA: *(Outraged.)* Talk of someone chasing after someone! I can't believe — after convincing me about how bad things are down there — I can't believe you'd consider some half-baked scheme of —

HONEY: It so happens his uncle's got an empty lot where we can put up banners like at the big places. And we'll be working together, building for the future.

LINDA: "Building for the future"? A quote from Curtis, I'll bet. He just wants to keep an eye on you. Also, he thinks Mississippi is a waste of time. You should find a boyfriend who's socially conscious, at least.

HONEY: Like Wes, who's so "socially conscious" he won't even try to hold your hand? Looks like you'll have to help him along, po' thing.

LINDA: *(Flustered.)* I keep telling you he's happy just being friends! *(She hurries to put the arm down on the record again.)* And so am I.

HONEY: Now give me some peace and quiet and let me get back to work.

LINDA: You want me to turn it off?

HONEY: Please!

LINDA: But killer Music 101! Followed by killer Philosophy 210! How are we ever gonna pass both of them?

HONEY: By doing one thing at a time. Or I can go over to the library.

LINDA: But Wes might come by.

HONEY: *(Looking at the clock.)* No men in the dorm past eleven. He doesn't have much time. Anyway, I don't have to be here.

LINDA: Yes, you do.

HONEY: So you can use me for a cover? I think Wesley Partridge is half the reason you're going to Mississippi.

LINDA: And Curtis Andrews is why you might not go! I'd be there even without Wes. I'm committed to the movement.

HONEY: And I'm committed to getting my work done. *(She jumps up, grabs her books, ready to leave. Linda lifts the arm from the record.)* Blessed silence. Thank you.

LINDA: How are we supposed to tell Ravel from Debussy, anyway? And Nietzsche from what's-his-name? This is gonna help me in government studies?

HONEY: "Government studies"? What happened to pre-law?

LINDA: Too narrow.

HONEY: So it's gone the way of pre-med and anthropology and Greco-Roman whatever-it-was and — ?

LINDA: They take too long. The bomb'll probably blow us up first anyway. Hiroshima . . . BOOM! Besides, we won't remember any of this stuff when we're forty!

HONEY: It's not supposed to be easy all the time, Lin. You're spoiled. Comes from being an only child, po' thing.

LINDA: What's with this "po' thing" every minute?

HONEY: Something my mama says.

LINDA: She doesn't talk like that.

HONEY: How do you know? You ever been down South?

LINDA: Florida.

HONEY: *Flahrida* doesn't count. Just wait till you get to Mississippi, Miss Subways. You and them speak a different tongue, 'specially the white ones.

LINDA: Not Wes. Not every white Southerner belongs to the Klan, you know.

HONEY: Wes doesn't count. He's from *North* Carolina. Kind of eccentric anyway. Like you.

LINDA: Look how she picks on me! And I was glad when I got you for a roommate!

HONEY: So you could show off how open-minded you are. The minute I saw you I knew you were a knee-jerk.

LINDA: I only stuck with you because of your yellow sweater.

HONEY: Your purple socks. "Damn if the girl ain't just my size," I thought, "Let me see what I can take advantage of."

LINDA: Of course, if I had your coloring I'd look much better in it.

HONEY: And if I had your hair I could toss my head around like a Breck commercial.

LINDA: The dean said, *(Nasally.)* "We'll stick the *colored* one and the *Jewish* one together so —"

HONEY: Look, shut up for ten minutes, then you can put Ravel back on and we'll trade your thin little Nietzsche for my big fat Descartes. *(Lifting a much thicker book.)*

LINDA: Deal.

THE PENETRATION PLAY
Winter Miller

Dramatic
Rain, late teens, early twenties; Maggie, forties

> *Rain is a friend of Maggie's daughter, Ash, with whom she is desperately in love. Ash has gone off on a date — with a boy. Rain tagged along, but left early and has come back to Maggie's house, where she is a guest. Maggie is unhappy in her marriage, and very vulnerable. Here, Rain comes on to her.*

RAIN: Maybe I'm too choosy. I get my mind stuck on one thing, and it's like blinders, you know, can't see the forest for the trees. And I'm persistent, you know, I can't give up without a fight. I'm tired of talking about me, let's go back to you.

MAGGIE: Now you're trying to bore us to death . . .

(Rain pours more wine.)

MAGGIE: No more, I'm going to be drunk any minute now.

RAIN: You'll be fine. Besides, there's nowhere you have to go, so why not give into Dionysus. Drink up . . .

MAGGIE: I like you, you're smart.

RAIN: Likewise.

(Rain raises her glass. Maggie follows suit.)

RAIN: To liking each other.

(They clink and drink.)

MAGGIE: Uh oh . . . I'm drunk. If I say something idiotic, don't hold it against me.

RAIN: I won't.

(Beat.)

MAGGIE: What?

RAIN: I'm waiting . . .

MAGGIE: For what?

RAIN: For you to say something idiotic!

MAGGIE: Probably everything I say is idiotic.

RAIN: I have a question.

MAGGIE: If I can answer it . . .

RAIN: How does your hair still look perfect?

MAGGIE: Are you kidding? It's a rat's nest I'm sure. Did I just say rat's nest? It's a bird's nest — see idiotic things come tripping off my tongue.

RAIN: No you can have a rat's nest.

MAGGIE: Thanks.

RAIN: No you don't — I meant it's not idiotic to say that.

MAGGIE: Oh.

RAIN: Not one is out of place . . .

(Rain reaches out to touch Maggie's hair. She removes her hand and Maggie sits back.)

MAGGIE: It's always neater when I get it blown out. Not that anyone EVER notices because we stay home and order pizza on a Saturday night when we're SUPPOSED to have dinner reservations. But yes, earlier this evening, my hair was presentable.

RAIN: You don't cut yourself any slack, do you?

MAGGIE: I'm too old for slack.

RAIN: When's the last time someone told you you were sexy?

MAGGIE: *(Giggles.)* Who can remember that far back?

RAIN: Honestly . . .

MAGGIE: I don't recall.

RAIN: I take it no one tells you on a daily basis?

MAGGIE: Ha!

RAIN: That's a shame. A lot of compliments have gone to waste.

(Rain pours the last of the wine into their glasses.)

MAGGIE: I cannot drink all that . . .

RAIN: Hush . . .

(Rain gently places her finger over Maggie's lips.)

RAIN: I want you to listen up.

MAGGIE: You're a talker once you get going!

RAIN: That's right. But listen, this is information I think you should hold onto.

MAGGIE: It's valuable is it?

RAIN: Yeah.

MAGGIE: After all this wine, I don't think I'll remember very much. I was nursing sherry before you stumbled home.

RAIN: Who's Sherry?

MAGGIE: What? Oh! You've got moxie.

RAIN: Are you going to listen to me . . . ?

MAGGIE: So serious! I'm all ears . . .

RAIN: You . . .

MAGGIE: Please let's not talk about me!

RAIN: Hush . . . *(Pause.)* You . . . are one of the sexiest women I have ever met.

MAGGIE: You're gonna make me blush! You're just crazy, that's what you are. *(Beat.)* Thank you. That's very sweet. And false.

RAIN: I wasn't finished, may I continue? I was about to say something nice . . .

MAGGIE: Proceed with your sweet lies . . .

RAIN: Do you remember when we met? You probably don't — it was a long time ago — First time, Ash and I came to visit, you were getting dressed so you didn't meet us at the door, you said hello from behind your bedroom door, and there was just this silky voice telling us to hurry up and dress for dinner. I didn't actually see you until we got to the restaurant. We walked in and you rose to greet us and I thought, who's this absolutely radiant woman? —

MAGGIE: Could have been one of my sisters —

RAIN: I'm not finished, sit tight — You had on a black low-cut dress with spaghetti straps that rested on those delicate collar bones, with your hair pulled back — and all I remember was — Catherine Deneuve — that's who you reminded me of — straight out of *Belle de Jour* — when he knocks on her door and she opens it with this naïve but resolved look — and she's just breathtaking —

MAGGIE: You're too much . . . You know that . . . ? My husband should hear you.

RAIN: Let's go tell him!

MAGGIE: Honey, he's out for the night. You could steamroll through the middle of his bed and he wouldn't stir. That was a beautiful night. I forgot you both came then . . .

RAIN: Thanks.

MAGGIE: I remember now that you say it. In my defense, there were all these people . . .

RAIN: You looked like you were on fire from the inside.

MAGGIE: You make me blush, I feel so silly. Here I am in my nightgown with a — how old are you, twenty something? — who's possibly saying the sweetest things I have not heard ANYONE say in years, and I'm drunk, and I'm blushing and I feel like I'm the one who's twenty-five years old, how about that?

(Rain reaches for Maggie and kisses her softly on the lips. Pause. Maggie pulls away.)

MAGGIE: Jesus Christ —

RAIN: You're beautiful.

MAGGIE: Please don't do that again.

RAIN: How can I help it?

(Rain kisses her.)

RAIN: How was that?

MAGGIE: My husband's right up those stairs.

RAIN: I forgot my steamroller.

MAGGIE: He could get up for a glass of water, or the bathroom.

RAIN: You are lovely. *(Beat.)* What are you waiting for?

MAGGIE: I can't do this. I don't do this. I wouldn't know the first thing.

RAIN: You can, see how easy it is . . . ?

MAGGIE: I have to go upstairs.

RAIN: But what you want is to stay right here. Maggie, I'm going to remind you what it feels like to be a woman.

(Rain kisses her. Maggie releases a faint moan and gives in, kissing her in return. They kiss. Rain slides her arms around Maggie and pulls her onto the couch.)

MAGGIE: *(Sitting up.)* I've had too much to drink. I don't know what I'm doing.

RAIN: *(Easing her down.)* I'll do everything.

MAGGIE: What are you going to do to me?

(Rain kisses her.)

MAGGIE: This isn't me.

RAIN: Close your eyes and lay back . . .

MAGGIE: What if —

RAIN: You worry too much.

(Rain kisses her down onto the couch.)

RAIN: You're beautiful. Put yourself in my hands.

MAGGIE: Turn off the light please.

(Rain turns off the light.)

THE PENETRATION PLAY
Winter Miller

Dramatic
Ash and Rain, late teens to early twenties

> *Rain and Ash have been best friends for years. Rain is desperately*
> *in love with Ash. Ash has just come home from a date — with a*
> *boy. It is late at night. Here, Rain comes clean about her feelings*
> *for Ash.*

ASH: Thanks for waiting up.

RAIN: How was your date?

MAGGIE: Why don't you invite Rich over and his parents?

ASH: Why don't you validate your existence separate from me!

MAGGIE: Alright Ashley — I was only — suggesting you invite them.

ASH: Get off my back!

MAGGIE: Rain, please wrap the cheese and put it in the cheese drawer on
the left. Good night.
(Maggie goes upstairs.)

ASH: Night.

RAIN: Good night.

ASH: I'm assuming this is my house because these are my keys and they
opened this door and that looked like my mother and you look like
my best friend, but other than that, I don't have a clue about what's
going on in this parafuckinglel universe.

RAIN: I'm exhausted . . .

ASH: Talk.

RAIN: Now you wanna talk?

ASH: Yeah, what the fuck?

RAIN: Sorry I missed dessert. Did you suck his dick?

ASH: *(Shoves Rain.)* Maybe . . .
(Beat.)

RAIN: *(Taking the cheese to the kitchen.)* Did you go all the way in the back of his car? I don't see grass stains on your ass — I'm assuming it was an indoor sports event?

ASH: You ran out —

RAIN: Here's forty bucks — if there's change / keep it.

ASH: You don't come back for ten minutes, then it's twenty — I called your cell —

RAIN: It was off. You called?

ASH: You didn't pick up.

(Rain checks her voice mail.)

RAIN: Four new messages. Are these all you?

ASH: It's me — obviously looking —

RAIN: Shhh — just a sec . . . .

(Thirty seconds pass as she listens to the message.)

RAIN: Listen to yourself! . . . I come out of the bathroom, you guys are making out — I figure you'd rather be alone —

ASH: You're a fucking piece of work.

RAIN: *(Sarcastic.)* Jeez, I had no idea you weren't having a good time. I'm sorry I left you alone — I thought you liked him.

ASH: I do —

RAIN: So, good, I was right. / You could thank me.

ASH: I come home and you . . .

RAIN: My head hurts. I had waaay too much wine. Your mom's cool to hang out with. Now I see where you got your sense of hum —

ASH: I'm not fucking around —

RAIN: Earlier was the fucking part of the evening. This is your afterglow. You don't seem like you're basking. "Cool black water — "

ASH: We didn't know where you were.

RAIN: If you were so worried, why didn't you just come home? *(Beat.)* 'Cause you figured, fuck it, she probably went home, so you parked in the Mercedes. Was it good or not?

ASH: That's such bullshit —

RAIN: Just tell me if it was good, I want to know if it was all worth it.

ASH: —

RAIN: That good . . . ?

ASH: If all what was worth it?

RAIN: You tell me.

ASH: I don't even know what you're talking about? I mean — what'd you do — run home to gossip with my mother — like a — like a little tattletale? What are you, six years old?

RAIN: I don't know why Maggie has it in her head you're going to fuck things up with Rich. She's convinced you lead everybody on and leave a trail of broken hearts. 'Cause, you know, I thought the trail was a very small trail — one, two people — that I could name. But she mentioned people I never heard of and I thought, here's my best friend but I don't know all this stuff?

ASH: She has no idea what she's talking about.

RAIN: She seems to know more than I do —

ASH: You even know I don't tell her —

RAIN: So how does she know all these other people? Who's Matt? Who's Charles?

ASH: What — does she keep a tally?

RAIN: Who are they?

ASH: I went out with them maybe twice.

RAIN: Did you fuck 'em?

ASH: Like I'm responsible to you? — You have a personal stake in who I'm —

RAIN: I'm your best friend, I care.

ASH: The way you always ask is overprotective — like you're passing judgment on me or who I'm with — so no I don't always tell you every little thing.

RAIN: When do I ever pass judgment?

ASH: You find something to pick out — about whoever — and —

RAIN: That's bullshit.

ASH: You do too! All the time.

RAIN: That's your opinion / it doesn't mean it's —

ASH: We're not even talking about this — you're an eel, you know that — how we go from talking about you to talking about me it's fucking slippery.

RAIN: I asked you one thing. Was he good?

ASH: It was amazing. Good enough for you? It was fucking great! We had a great time, he's great, we're great, it was all great!

RAIN: Did he stick his finger in your ass?

ASH: I'm going to bed.

RAIN: Did you come at least?

(Ashley lunges at Rain. Taking her by surprise and pushing her onto the chair.)

RAIN: Whoa — 'Cause I know sometimes it's hard for you to just give in —

ASH: You're jealous.

RAIN: Am I?

ASH: *(Pinning Rain, who isn't struggling.)* Admit it. Go ahead, say it.

(Beat.)

RAIN: There is something I have to tell you . . . *(Dramatic pause.)* Your leg is on my bracelet, which is crushing my wrist —

ASH: Good.

RAIN: Well, it hurts.

ASH: Poor baby.

RAIN: I'm serious.

ASH: That's unfortunate, isn't it.

(Beat.)

RAIN: Otherwise, this is nice, you on top. I don't know why I always pictured you on the bottom.

ASH: Yeah? You think about it?

RAIN: Yeah. You?

(Ashley hovers above Rain. Slowly she drops her pelvis into Rain's.)

ASH: You want it?

RAIN: You're asking me?

ASH: You wanna feel me? . . . How's that feel.

RAIN: You're a natural.

(They are close.)

RAIN: I have one question . . .

ASH: You wanna kiss me?

RAIN: Are you thinking of me or remembering Rich?

ASH: What do you think?

(Beat.)

RAIN: I think . . . You resemble your mother.

ASH: What if I put my hand here . . . ? *(She rubs Rain's breast.)* What about here? *(She rubs Rain's crotch.)*

RAIN: You come across as a very sweet girl.

ASH: Well, I am.

RAIN: But this is definitely your sexier side.

ASH: How do you like it?

(Rain sits up, throws Ashley off her, taunting. Rain is over Ashley now.)

RAIN: What is it? All those glasses of wine and lover boy still can't relax you? You still can't quite get off? You gotta come home and "wrestle" with me?

ASH: Fuck you.

RAIN: That's what I'm here for.

ASH: Is that all?

(Ashley pushes Rain over.)

RAIN: Let me know when you come, I'll be right beneath you.

ASH: You wish you could make me come.

RAIN: I have no doubt I can . . . Ask your mother.

(Ashley lunges at Rain. Knocking her violently to the ground. Rain lays motionless.)

ASH: Hey — OK stop fucking with me . . . You get an Oscar. Get up. It's not funny. It's not. I'm not laughing . . . C'mon. Fine. I'm going up to bed.

(Ashley gets up to leave, gets to the stairs, Rain still hasn't moved so she comes back and pokes her.)

ASH: Hey.

(Ashley bends over Rain, more concerned.)

ASH: Rain . . . Hey. Are you OK? Rain . . . , hey? C'mon . . . Rain . . .

(Rain bolts up and kicks Ashley over and is instantly on top of her.)

ASH: You're such a fucking asshole! Let me up!

(Rain leans down as if to kiss her, and hovers right above her lips.)

RAIN: I got a question . . .

ASH: Get the fuck off!

RAIN: Did you come?

ASH: Get off me.

RAIN: Still not yet? You are tough.

(Ashley spits in Rain's face.)

RAIN: You wanna swap spit?

(Beat. Rain leans back and begins to type on Ashley's chest as before.)

RAIN: Dear —

ASH: What's wrong with you?

RAIN: Ooh I wish I had Wite-Out.

> *(Starting over.)*
> My Dearest Ashley,
> *(Ding!) (Slap.)*
> While you were out on your date
> *(Ding!) (Slap.)*
> With the man of your mother's dreams . . .
> *(Ding!) (Slap.)*

ASH: Get off me.

RAIN: Not done with the letter . . .

> *(Resumes typing.)*
> I came home and . . .
> *(Ding!) (Slap.)*
> Are you ready for this?
> *(Ding!) (Slap.)*

ASH: Fuck you.

RAIN: *(Types.)* I came home to find your very pretty mother

> *(Ding!) (Slap.)*
> in her very sexy nightgown
> *(Ding!) (Slap.)*
> and your very sexy mother and I
> *(Ding!) (Slap.)*
> sat on the couch with a bottle of wine . . .
> *(Ding!) (Slap.)*
> and some fancy cheese.
> *(Ding!) (Slap.)*
> And we drank our wine.
> *(Ding!) (Slap.)*
> And we ate our cheese.
> *(Ding!) (Slap.)*
> And I —

> *(Ash grabs Rain, pulling herself to Rain's lips and kisses her. Beat.)*

RAIN: P.S. But I was thinking of you.

> *(They kiss. Rain spits in her hand and forcefully reaches down Ashley's pants. Pause. They kiss, a combination of desire and aggression.)*

RED DEATH
Lisa D'Amour

Dramatic
Jane Withers, thirties; Lucinda Albright, seventeen

> *Jane and Lucinda are in a dance club in Barcelona. Jane has been tracking Lucinda's father, Prospero, for many years, with the intention of killing him.*

JANE: Do you think he transcended their death?

LUCINDA: My father?

JANE: Just curious.

LUCINDA: No. If anything he DEscended.

JANE: Maybe you should stay here. In Barcelona.

LUCINDA: Are you staying?

JANE: If you stay, I will.

> *(Quickly, another bass-heavy vibration. Lucinda almost falls to the floor. She rights herself as the music resumes.)*

LUCINDA: What did you say?

JANE: I said I'll be here two more weeks. To finish my course. But maybe you should stay. Get some kind of student visa. Get a job teaching English, or giving tours.

LUCINDA: God, I couldn't pull that off.

JANE: Why not?

LUCINDA: Look, I've never had a job in my life. I suck as much money out of my parents as I can and spend it like water flushed down the toilet. Why worry when there's always more? There's plenty of everything to go around. I have a different set of friends every week and I fuck them over too, sometimes, if I get in a mood. I dance and I dance and I dance and I dance and I see the downward slope and I am not afraid *(A look to Jane: a test.)* I'm not afraid of the Panel.

JANE: What?

LUCINDA: I said I'm not afraid of the Panel.

JANE: I'm sorry I don't know what you are talking about.

LUCINDA: I said I'm not in any fucking hurry to grow old.

JANE: But you're nineteen years old. You're going to have to take charge of your life sometime.

LUCINDA: Look, who are you? Why do you care? What were you doing when you were nineteen years old?

JANE: I was looking for your father.

LUCINDA: What?

JANE: I was looking for your father.

(Another bass-heavy vibration. Lucinda falls flat on the floor. Jane helps her up.)

LUCINDA: How do you know my father?

JANE: What?

LUCINDA: You said you were looking for my father.

JANE: I did not.

LUCINDA: Yes you did.

JANE: Lucinda. Lucinda. Lucinda. Snap out of it. Enjoy yourself. Who's your father?

LUCINDA: Prospero Albright. He's an international consultant and a rank, stinking hole. He thinks he knows everything.

JANE: But he doesn't.

LUCINDA: No he doesn't.

JANE: Because he is short-sighted and obsessed with the specifics of his highly specialized field.

LUCINDA: How did you know?

JANE: Most fathers are. And most fathers worry when their daughters are out alone, in the dead of night, in a strange country.

LUCINDA: He knows better than to try and stop me. It's not like I have an example to follow. Mom may have had a chance if she hadn't met Dad. But it's too late for her now, right? And Dad, Jesus, that fucking enigma. One night he's bawling his eyes out, writing multiple checks to the fucking Save the Historic Oak Fund, the next night he's sneaking into my room in the dead of night, asking if I'd like to try a little bit of the white powder he brought back special from Milan. Just a wee bit, you know, to take the edge off, a father/daughter thing . . . Don't be shocked.

JANE: I'm . . . I'm not.

LUCINDA: Sure you are.

(A moment of total clarity for Lucinda.)

I am a conduit for hate. I feel it pushing up through the ground. I feel it circulate through my body and exit through the tips of my fingers. It's why I am on this earth. I've felt it ever since I was a child.

JANE: Why? Why do you think you have felt it?

(Lucinda begins to shake. A terrifying revelation drops into her head.)

LUCINDA: I'm afraid it runs in my family.

(Another bass-heavy drone. Lucinda does not waver. Neither does Jane. They look into each other's eyes.)

LUCINDA: You're with them, aren't you?

JANE: Yes.

LUCINDA: Oh fuck. You're here to kill me.

(Music. Lucinda makes a drugged, half-assed attempt to run. Jane catches her, holds her. She takes off Lucinda's mask. Lucinda takes off Jane's mask.)

LUCINDA: Oh, shit.

JANE: What?

LUCINDA: I knew I knew you. My father keeps a picture of you in his red box of files.

JANE: *(Too loud:)* How did you get in there? How? Did he give you a key?

LUCINDA: No. I gave him a hand job.

(Jane is so shocked she drops Lucinda to the floor. Then, she gathers her back up. Lucinda looks into her eyes.)

LUCINDA: I'm lying.

No I'm not.

I'm lying.

No I'm not.

Everybody's got it in them, everybody. You should know that.

How am I going to die?

JANE: The drugs will be taking effect any moment now. You won't feel a thing.

LUCINDA: I was doomed from the beginning.

JANE: Yes. But now you're free.

(Lucinda faints in Jane's arms. Jane carries her off.)

SCHOOLGIRL FIGURE
Wendy MacLeod

Seriocomic
Renee, an anorexic, seventeen; Patty, a bulimic, seventeen

> *Setting: Monique's hospital room. In this scene, the reigning Car-*
> *penter Queen, Monique, has just died, leaving the field open for*
> *Renee, who wants to win the Carpenter crown and The Bradley,*
> *Monique's trophy boyfriend.*

RENEE: Come on, let's go.

PATTY: *Renee.*

RENEE: What?

PATTY: She's *dead.*

RENEE: So?

PATTY: We can't just walk out.

RENEE: What are we gonna do? Embalm her?

PATTY: We should close her eyes or something.

RENEE: Go ahead.

PATTY: I don't want to touch a dead girl!

RENEE: We have to tell The Bradley. Console him.

PATTY: I'm gonna pull the blanket up.

RENEE: Whatever. Wait.

PATTY: What?

RENEE: That's a cute necklace.
    (Patty slaps her hand.)
    Ow! Like she's gonna know the difference.

PATTY: The Bradley probably gave it to her.

RENEE: I'll just say she gave it to me. Damn. I can't get the clasp undone.

PATTY: I'll *buy* you a necklace.

RENEE: I've never seen a necklace like this.

PATTY: My God Renee, her body's still warm!

RENEE: *(Touching Monique:)* Tepid.

(Renee yanks the necklace.)

There.

(Monique makes a final cry and collapses. The machines flatline and beep.)

PATTY: Oh my God you strangled her!

RENEE: You can't strangle a corpse!

PATTY: She wasn't dead yet! She just made a noise!

RENEE: That was a death rattle. Didn't you read *How We Die?*

PATTY: No. Did you?

RENEE: I read the book jacket. I was looking for tips.

PATTY: Renee!

RENEE: Look, if she wasn't dead then, she is now.

PATTY: How can we be sure?

RENEE: Look.

(Renee shakes her and she's all floppy.)

PATTY: Stop that!

RENEE: Why? She's a corpse!

PATTY: You have to treat a body with respect.

RENEE: I have total respect for Monique. But it's time to look to the future.

PATTY: She was our friend.

RENEE: Oh she was not.

PATTY: She was our acquaintance! You were always talking about what an inspiration she was!

RENEE: Look, make new friends and lose the old, one is silver and the other's gold.

PATTY: But old friends are the ones who are gold.

RENEE: No they're not, they're silver.

PATTY: They are so gold. And gold is worth way more than silver!

RENEE: I can't wear gold I'm a summer!

PATTY: Would you be like this if I died?

RENEE: You're not gonna die, you eat like a horse.

PATTY: Well if you died would you like me to be all . . . *(Shakes Monique.)*

RENEE: What I'd like you to do is cry.

PATTY: I will.

RENEE: Now.

PATTY: Why?

RENEE: *The Bradley's* out there. We have to look in need of consolation.

PATTY: I am in need of consolation. I'm on a total bummer.

RENEE: Oh get over yourself and cry. Think about me for once in your life. What kind of bitch will I look like if I'm not bummed over Monique's death?

PATTY: A total bitch.

RENEE: See?

PATTY: Boo-hoo. Boo-hoo.

RENEE: "Boo-hoo? Boo-hoo?"

PATTY: Well *I* don't know how to fake it.

RENEE: Get your nose red and snotty.

PATTY: Are you going to get *your* nose red and snotty?

RENEE: No, I'm going to catch my breath . . . like this.

PATTY: Can't I do that?

RENEE: No, it will look totally fake. No two people cry the same way.

PATTY: Well *you* take the snotty way.

RENEE: Perhaps you didn't understand what I said. *The Bradley's* out there.

PATTY: Maybe we could *make* ourselves cry. By using The Method. Mrs. Blue showed us how in Drama class.

RENEE: What method?

PATTY: The acting Method. Like you think of really sad things.

RENEE: I missed the Barney's after-Christmas sale when we were away.

PATTY: That's not *sad.*

RENEE: It was *so* sad. I've *never* missed the after-Christmas sale before. I *begged* my mother to come back early but she wouldn't. There was like all this new powder and she *wouldn't.* By the time I got there it was like all picked over, and all that was left was the zeroes and the fourteens and the *orange* things.

PATTY: That is not sad. I mean think about Monique's parents. Her parents are gonna be really sad.

RENEE: She's *got* a sister. I mean, they have a *spare.*

PATTY: Still. She used to be their little baby.

RENEE: Babies are *fat.*

PATTY: They're never gonna see her graduate from high school or get married or . . .

RENEE: Would you stop? You're totally depressing me.

PATTY: I'm trying to make myself cry. *(Renee slaps her.)* Owww. That hurt.

RENEE: That's the Renee method.

SCHOOLGIRL FIGURE
Wendy MacLeod

Seriocomic

Renee, seventeen, an anorexic; Patty, seventeen, her best friend, a bulimic

> *Renee has a diabolical plan to become the skinniest by tempting her*
> *anorexic rival Jeanine with David's cookies. Patty is starting to doubt*
> *the wisdom of the entire competition.*

> *(An awning unfurls that says David's Cookies. Patty and Renee enter,*
> *Renee on a motorized cart.)*

PATTY: Look where you're going Renee. You ran into a stroller in the food court. That baby is going to need stitches.

RENEE: Oh, babies always find something to cry about.

PATTY: Let's wait in front of that fan that blows the cookie smell.

RENEE: Are you crazy? There's airborne calories!

PATTY: Wouldn't it be weird if David were in the back baking cookies and he came out and we fell in love?

RENEE: David who?

PATTY: *David.* David of the Cookies.

RENEE: Yeah, and Mrs. Fields could be your maid of honor. Not.

PATTY: I mean who was David? They never show you a picture of David.

RENEE: There is no David.

PATTY: How do you know?

RENEE: There is no anybody. Aunt Jemima. Betty Crocker.

PATTY: There's an Ann Landers.

RENEE: There's an Ann Landers *factory.* A bunch of little know-nothings answer those letters. "Seek counseling." I could tell you that.

PATTY: Maybe you should.

RENEE: Maybe I should what?

PATTY: Seek counseling.

RENEE: Why? So some fat woman wearing organic cotton can tell me I have body image problems? Well maybe I do. But I'd rather have that than body problems any day.

PATTY: You should really think about the media's role in this.

RENEE: We're supposed to take a number.

PATTY: I mean all the magazines have thin models, all the movies have thin actresses. . .

RENEE: Who wants to look at fat models? Who wants to watch a bunch of flabby movie stars jiggling around? Of course the media has a role in this. Thank God. Somebody's upholding standards.

PATTY: Which kind are you going to get?

RENEE: The fattening kind. Where the hell is the cookie girl?

PATTY: Are you going to have one?

RENEE: Me? As if.

PATTY: Can I have one?

RENEE: The cookies are for Jeanine.

PATTY: What if Jeanine doesn't eat them?

RENEE: She will. She has a thing for cookies. My brother worked at 7-11 and she was in there all the time making Pepperidge Farm runs.

PATTY: That was me.

RENEE: It was her too. Before she went anorexic. Hello?!

PATTY: But she won't go up an entire size just from eating a bag of cookies.

RENEE: Well it won't just be the cookies. She'll feel so ashamed she'll binge.

PATTY: What if she throws them all up?

RENEE: She's not a spewer. I've seen her try. She has a lazy gag reflex.

PATTY: Some people just don't have what it takes.

RENEE: We'll smear chocolate at the corner of our lips. We'll tell her we went on a total macadamia binge. Then she'll think she has a calorie cushion and she'll binge.

PATTY: Well if I'm gonna say I binged, why can't I binge?

RENEE: This is not about you. The whole world doesn't revolve around you. It revolves around me. And Jeanine is in my way.

PATTY: If this were a musical, this is where you'd break into song.

RENEE: Where'd you learn that? In Mrs. Blue's drama class?

PATTY: Yeah.

RENEE: Isn't she the one who said her husband liked her love handles?

PATTY: Yeah.

RENEE: Stay far, far away from that woman. She's out of her mind.

PATTY: She was in a class with Marlon Brando once. And they were all
like doing an improv and you had to guess what everybody was and
he was doing the pom-pom on the tip of a sultan's slipper and he
was such a good actor that everybody guessed!

RENEE: Those classes are rotting your brain.

PATTY: You should go to class.

RENEE: I went to gym the day they had the caliper test!

PATTY: That doesn't count!

RENEE: I was in my very own percentile.

PATTY: You should go to the classes with books!

RENEE: I don't want my brain to get fat. C'mon, let's go to Mrs. Fields.

SECOND
Neal Utterback

Dramatic
Lauren and Vick, thirties

> *Lauren is a successful New York surgeon and Vick's partner. Vick
> is a no-nonsense reporter who is spinning her wheels in her career.
> Lauren has just returned home after the death of her mother. This
> is the first time we see them together. Vick is working on an as-
> signment to track down a mysterious, unidentified man who only
> two weeks ago performed what some claim was a miracle.*

VICK: How was the funeral?

LAUREN: Wonderful. There were clowns and pony rides.

VICK: Did you have cotton candy?

LAUREN: And elephant ears, I won't eat for a week.

VICK: I'm a shit, I'm sorry.

LAUREN: Yes, you are.

VICK: You must be exhausted.

LAUREN: I feel like I've been on a plane all year.

VICK: Well, you have been, pretty much. Why don't you take some time
off from the hospital? Don't they owe you some bereavement. for
God's sake?

LAUREN: I have to go in tonight.

VICK: It's Christmas Eve.

LAUREN: I told Sarah I'd cover for her. Her daughter's in some Christmas
pageant, playing an ox or . . .

VICK: Lauren, you're exhausted.

LAUREN: I know. I haven't had my period for — I don't even remember
how long.

VICK: You're stressed out, honey. Flying back and forth for eight months —

LAUREN: Nine.

VICK: *Nine* months, dealing with your mother, keeping your patient load, it's bound to catch up with you.

LAUREN: Mom didn't even know who we were those last days.

VICK: Who?

LAUREN: What?

VICK: We who?

LAUREN: We who what?

VICK: You said your mother didn't know who "we" were.

LAUREN: Did I? Huh.

VICK: I would have come, Lauren. I'm just not good —

LAUREN AND VICK: — with death.

LAUREN: Because I'm great with it. The hours of sobbing — the salt from the tears is a natural exfoliate giving your skin that red, puffy look that's in all the magazines.

(Vick's phone rings.)

VICK: Lover, I'm sorry. *(Vick answers the phone.)* Hey, Maggie, you old dyke. *(To Lauren.)* It's Maggie. *(Into the phone.)* Well, thank you, Merry Christmas to you. Lauren says Merry — Uh huh . . . uh huh . . . oh no . . . oh no! *(To Lauren.)* Little Joey got food poisoning at Maggie's mother's house and the next day threw up on Santa at Macy's. *(Into the phone.)* I tell you, Margaret, I do not know why you raise a child in this city. It's unsanitary.

LAUREN: The city or the child?

VICK: Yeah, she just got home. She's a trooper. Of course, I'll tell her. Listen, let me go. I'll call you about New Year's. Yeah, OK, hot stuff, you have a good one. We love you. Give Joey a kiss . . . after you wipe him down. Uh huh, bye-bye. *(To Lauren.)* The phone calls, my God. You'd think it was Christmas. Maggie sends her condolences. What were you saying?

LAUREN: I needed you there.

VICK: Where?

LAUREN: Mom's funeral.

VICK: Lauren, God knows I'm sorry about your mother, but I have been extremely busy. And not like "I was washing my hair" busy, I mean — *(Can't find the word.)* Aarg! You've been gone for eight months and/

LAUREN: /Nine.

VICK: Nine, whatever, a long time. You knew it was coming. And you weren't even close to the woman.

LAUREN: Still.

VICK: I can't handle that much . . . emotion. Besides, most of the time your mother hated me, so my absence was hardly a loss to her. And. sweetie, she didn't much care for you either. And I hate being put in the position where I am supposed to feel or act a certain way and then feel guilty if I don't. *And* I can't look at dead people.

LAUREN: She was cremated.

VICK: . . . Well . . . she *was* good at saving space. I'm glad you're back.

LAUREN: Me too.

VICK: Merry Christmas.

LAUREN: Merry Christmas.

VICK: This snow, my God, can you believe it?

LAUREN: What's to believe?

VICK: What happened to global warming?

LAUREN: We'll have to work harder to destroy the planet.

VICK: Oh, speaking of phone calls.

LAUREN: Thought we were talking about snow.

VICK: Who calls me yesterday?

LAUREN: The Pope.

VICK: Barbara fucking Walters.

LAUREN: I was close.

VICK: Wishes me happy holidays and congrats on the orphanage scoop, which Prescott said was human interest fluff.

LAUREN: That actually . . . I need to tell you some/

VICK: /I'm sorry but this whole thing is just eating me up. This is the second bogus assignment I've had in as many months. Prescott is trying to crucify me, I swear to God.

LAUREN: What if it's true?

VICK: The Miracle Man? Are you kidding? It's not even worth my abilities. The enlightened-but-crazy-bum-turned-savior-thing is so overdone. What's worse is, I can't win. I look like the bad guy, or worse. the idiot, regardless of how I approach the story. If I discredit him at Christmas time, I look like some typical loudmouthed atheist cynic, which I am, but still not a good career move. And if I allude to the possibility that it could be true, then it will look like I believe him, like I support this nut, and what intelligent person would believe a story like that? I know, I know, why not just be impartial? But come on, that's just not realistic. The whole city is crazy about this. I'm sorry, I don't mean crazy like —

LAUREN: The last thing Mom said to me was that I should have a child.

VICK: . . . I take it back, I do mean "crazy."

LAUREN: She was quoting Revelations and speaking in Latin.

VICK: Judith spoke Latin?

LAUREN: No. I mean, yes she was speaking Latin but she couldn't before. The cancer spread, it developed into lesions on her temporal lobe.

VICK: Is that bad?

LAUREN: Well . . . she's dead. She was having hallucinations. She would talk to God.

VICK: Did God talk back?

LAUREN: They had tea together every day. Apparently, God is a terrible bore. He goes on and on about the Coming.

VICK: Is that a euphemism?

LAUREN: And God talks about His guilt and regret regarding His children.

VICK: So, God is a he?

LAUREN: Well, actually, no, God is an androgynous, iridescent Jell-O mold.

VICK: I knew it.

LAUREN: Mom wouldn't take her medication so when she would have these seizures — she was blissfully happy. I mean, Vicky, you can't imagine her conviction, it was impressive and . . . enviable. I've never believed anything that much.

VICK: I wonder if all religious zealots really are crazy.

LAUREN: She wasn't . . . well, OK, she was crazy.

VICK: If you take every religious fanatic — would they all test positive for some neurological or chemical imbalance?

LAUREN: Is true faith only possible — can you only believe in the ethereal when the physical fails?

VICK: Maybe this Miracle Man is reducible to a few synaptic misfires. Ooh, maybe that's my angle.

LAUREN: But is it totally impossible for it to be true? I mean, maybe Mom's visions — the, the lesions gave her sight — that she could see things to which we have become blind.

VICK: Honey, your mother was obviously expressing guilt over her own misguided parenting.

LAUREN: And you said this Miracle Man isn't even the one claiming this event is true.

VICK: No, it's the rest of the city; he's not saying anything.

LAUREN: But isn't that faith? What does it take to believe in something beyond your understanding?

VICK: Apparently, a swift whack to the temples does the trick.

LAUREN: Sometimes, I want so desperately to have religion, to believe in . . . anything. Part of me was so jealous of my mother. Just to know the sheer bliss of belief — even in a Jell-O mold.

VICK: I think we still have a little fruit cup in the fridge. You wanna . . .

LAUREN: She spoke Latin.

VICK: How do you know it was Latin?

LAUREN: It was Latin.

VICK: Maybe it wasn't your mother *speaking* Latin but you *hearing* Latin.

LAUREN: That's my point. What if the lesions weren't a manifestation of the cancer spreading but a result of a genetic vulnerability? What if I have a predestined, preprogrammed genetic proclivity to either cancer or, specifically, temporal lobe damage? How would I know if I was hallucinating if I believe what I see to be true? And maybe that doesn't matter. I'd lose my job, my social standing; I'd be an outcast —

VICK: — But happy?

LAUREN: But blissfully happy.

VICK: I'll visit you in the asylum.

LAUREN: Maybe you do have to lose everything before you find yourself.

VICK: If you keep thinking about it, you'll make it happen. Power of suggestion.

LAUREN: Mother would talk about a sensation in her stomach, like riding a roller-coaster and that would spread into a warm, tingly feeling over her entire body. Then she would have these spontaneous, intense surges of *joy* and sadness, confusing and wonderful. And that's how she knew *It* was around.

VICK: God?

LAUREN: God.

VICK: The Jell-O mold?

LAUREN: And she would hear music.

VICK: Like a choir of angels? Harps and eunuchs?

LAUREN: James Brown.

VICK: James Brown?

LAUREN AND VICK: The Godfather of Soul.

VICK: A method to her madness.

LAUREN: And that's what scares me, Vick, because lately — lately, I hear music.

[*(John enters through stage right doorway and crosses to the window.)*]

VICK: James Brown?

LAUREN: Christmas carols.

VICK: OK, Lauren, it's Christmas.

LAUREN: No, in my head, I hear Christmas carols.

TWO SISTERS AND A PIANO
Nilo Cruz

Dramatic
Maria Celia, thirty-six; Sofia, twenty-four

This play takes place in 1991, during the Pan-American games in Cuba. Maria, a novelist, and Sofia, a pianist, are sisters, serving time under house arrest.

(Daytime. Soft, grayish white lights. It is raining outside. Maria Celia is reciting a letter to her husband.)

MARIA CELIA: "My dear love: It's no longer a secret, the Ministry is holding up your letters. Every part of me, even my fury and rancor, is being registered and kept in a file. Now they're keeping your letters to document the weight of my heart. Today when I woke up and washed my face . . . " *(Touches her face.)* "I thought that perhaps when you see me again, I'll be less than you expected, that you'll find me less beautiful. I'm thirty-six years old and I feel my life is evaporating in front of me, that I'm rotting and decaying in this house . . . It's the thought of you, the strength of your eyes that brings the precipitation of life . . . I kiss you all over, Maria Celia . . . " *(Lights up on Sofia knitting.)*

SOFIA: We're almost out of the good yarn.

MARIA CELIA: What's wrong with this other yarn?

SOFIA: It's tough on my hands. It's like steel wool for scouring pots. You start weaving and purling with that thing and you'll end up with minced meat for hands.

MARIA CELIA: That's the only yarn we have left.

SOFIA: I have to protect my hands.

MARIA CELIA: Use a pair of gloves. If we don't knit there won't be any bedspreads. And if there's no bedspreads, what are we going to give Cirilo to sell?

SOFIA: It's days like this I could play the piano the whole day.

MARIA CELIA: I bet. You tell me that every day.

SOFIA: I can't play it anymore. The piano is falling apart.

MARIA CELIA: What about the permit you got to have it tuned?

SOFIA: I sent for a piano tuner — hasn't shown up.

MARIA CELIA: Give it some time.

SOFIA: Look at my hands, veins starting to show up from all this knitting. That's always been my fear. On men the veins look good. On men yes — because it makes them look strong and virile, like their plumbing works well and lots of blood flows through all their parts. I hate these needles. I hate all this knitting.

MARIA CELIA: I know. You tell me every time we knit.

SOFIA: Oscarito had lots of veins like a Roman aqueduct. Everywhere. I loved how they showed his strength. All the rivers from his heart. Oh, I wish I had a glass of rum with ice. A man . . . A man, is what I wish I had . . . I loved doing it when it rained. *(Stretches.)*

MARIA CELIA: You sound like a cat in heat.

SOFIA: Take a break for God's sake! I don't know where you get all that energy, when all we had to eat were eggs and mangoes.

MARIA CELIA: I'm tired but I keep at it. I keep at it.

SOFIA: If that lieutenant comes again you should ask him if he could get us something to eat.

MARIA CELIA: I told you I'm not going to ask him for food.

SOFIA: Why not? He could make life easier for us.

MARIA CELIA: No. I've been thinking of having him read me the letters and that's all. I'm not going to give him any papers. I'm just going to tell him the story.

SOFIA: I wouldn't do it. He'll find something in it. It always happens.

MARIA CELIA: What could he possibly find? It's a simple love story, for God's sake!

SOFIA: He could testify against you. You keep me out of it.

MARIA CELIA: Keep you out of it and you want me to ask him for food!

SOFIA: Well, we have it bad as it is. I don't want anything else to do with your writing.

MARIA CELIA: I can't believe the things that come out of your mouth! You might as well turn me in.

SOFIA: I can't go back to the prison! Not back there, you hear me . . . I'd rather be in a hole, underground, full of worms. Every night I have nightmares about that place. I wake up out of breath, like a lost animal . . .

MARIA CELIA: Forget I said anything. Do you remember when you were playing that song on the piano?

SOFIA: Which one?

MARIA CELIA: "La Savane." *(The music of Gottschalk is heard.)* I'd never heard it that way before. The whole music . . . I felt as if I had to leave my body. I went to the sea. Next minute, I was writing about this man and this woman in the marina. The story had gotten inside me like a sickness. For three days I stayed up at night writing.

SOFIA: Are you the woman in this story?

MARIA CELIA: No.

SOFIA: And him?

MARIA CELIA: He's like the man next door.

SOFIA: The man next door? Why him?

MARIA CELIA: I don't know. It all came to me that day.

The woman in the story goes to visit him at the marina when he's on duty. She always tells him that she wants to know about the sea . . . She wants to learn from him. The first night she goes to him, she asks if he eats alone, and he tells her that he does. She tells him it's sad to see men having dinner alone. A person should never eat alone. She asks him if she could cook for him. That they could have dinner together overlooking the sea.

SOFIA: Does he accept?

MARIA CELIA: He's not allowed to receive visitors when he's on duty. But she tells him that she wouldn't be a visitor, she'd only come to bring him food.

SOFIA: That'd be something I would say. And I would show up to see him even if he said no. I'd show up in a white dress.

MARIA CELIA: She wears a white dress.

SOFIA: Maybe a long blue scarf, to go with the sea, white sandals and a parasol.

MARIA CELIA: It's nighttime, Sofie. Why would she have a parasol?

SOFIA: That's true. You said it was nighttime. I'm sorry. You took me there with the story. *(Laughs.)* — Do you realize this is going to be another summer that we won't be able to go to the sea?

MARIA CELIA: Yes. I know.

SOFIA: I was sitting there with him at the marina with a picnic basket. My feet dangling from the pier . . . And me occasionally dipping my toes in the water, then looking at him.

MARIA CELIA: They meet on a tower, Sofie. A glass tower and it's not a picnic.

SOFIA: Go on. Don't mind me. I'm making your story into something else.

MARIA CELIA: Now I forgot where I was.

SOFIA: The glass tower.

MARIA CELIA: Yes, the glass tower surrounded by blue boats. . . Fishermen retrieving their nets from the sea. Seagulls.

SOFIA: Yes, lots of seagulls.

MARIA CELIA: The woman walks by the sea taking puffs from her cigarette, leaving smoke behind like a steamship. She climbs the stairs to the glass tower. She goes to see him, with her purse full of bread, rice, plantains, beans, boiled eggs, avocados, guava marmalade, napkins, forks, spoons, salt and pepper. A whole restaurant in her little bag.

SOFIA: That should be the name of the story: "Picnic by the Light of the Moon." I guess you can tell him all about it. What could be wrong with a picnic in a marina? But don't show him any writing.

ANNA IN THE TROPICS. © 2003 by Nilo Cruz. Reprinted by permission of Peregrine Whittlesey, 279 Central Park W., New York, NY 10024. The entire text has been published in an acting edition by Dramatists Play Service, which handles performance rights. Contact: Dramatists Play Service, 440 Park Ave. S., New York, NY 10016, www.dramatists.com, 212-MU3-8960.

BIG OLE WASHING MACHINE. © 2004 by Stephen Belber. Reprinted by permission of Playscripts, Inc. The entire text has been published in an acting edition by Playscripts, Inc., which also handles performance rights. Contact: Playscripts, Inc., Box 237060, New York, NY 10023, www.playscripts.com, 866-NEW-PLAY.

THE BRIGHTEST LIGHT. © 2004 by Diana Howie. Reprinted by permission of Playscripts, Inc., which has published the entire text in an acting edition and which handles performance rights. Contact: Playscripts, Inc., Box 237060, New York, NY 10023, www.playscripts.com, 866-NEW-PLAY.

BRIGHT IDEAS. © 2004 by Eric Coble. Reprinted by permission of Val Day, William Morris Agency, Inc., 1325 Ave. of the Americas, New York, NY 10019. The entire text has been published in an acting edition by Dramatists Play Service, which handles performance rights. Contact: Dramatists Play Service, 440 Park Ave. S., New York, NY 10016, www.dramatists.com, 212-MU3-8960.

BUICKS. © 2003 by Julian Sheppard. Reprinted by permission of Michael Cardonick, Creative Artists Agency, 162 Fifth Ave., New York, NY 10010. The entire text has been published in an acting edition by Dramatists Play Service, which handles performance rights. Contact: Dramatists Play Service, 440 Park Ave. S., New York, NY 10016, www.dramatists.com, 212-MU3-8960.

COMMON GROUND. © 2004 by Brendon Votipka. Reprinted by permission of Playscripts, Inc., which has published the entire text in an acting edition and which handles performance rights. Contact: Playscripts, Inc., Box 237060, New York, NY 10023, www.playscripts.com, 866-NEW-PLAY.

CRASHING THE GATE. © 2004 by Frederick Stroppel. Reprinted by permission of the author. The entire text has been published in an acting edition by Samuel French, Inc. (in *Kidney Stones*), which also handles performance rights. Contact: Samuel French, Inc., 45 W. 25th St., New York, NY 10010, www.samuelfrench.com, 212-206-8990.

ELOISE & RAY. © 2005 by Stephanie Fleischmann. Reprinted by permission of Playscripts, Inc. The entire text has been published in an acting edition by Playscripts, Inc., which also handles performance rights. Contact: Playscripts, Inc., Box 237060, New York, NY 10023, www.playscripts.com, 866-NEW-PLAY.

PLAY IT AS IT LIES. © 2004 by Granville Wyche Burgess. Reprinted by permission of Playscripts, Inc., which has published the entire text in an acting edition and which handles performance rights. Contact: Playscripts, Inc., Box 237060, New York, NY 10023, www.playscripts.com, 866-NEW-PLAY.

PURE CONFIDENCE. © 2005 by Carlyle Brown. Reprinted by permission of Bret Adams Ltd., 448 W. 44th St., New York, NY 10036. The entire text has been published by Smith and Kraus in *Humana Festival 2005: The Complete Plays.* Contact Bret Adams Ltd. for performance rights.

RED DEATH. © 2004 by Lisa D'Amour. Reprinted by permission of Playscripts, Inc., which has published the entire text in an acting edition and which handles performance rights. Contact: Playscripts, Inc., Box 237060, New York, NY 10023, www.playscripts.com, 866-NEW-PLAY.

THE RETURN TO MORALITY. © 2004 by Jamie Pachino. Reprinted by permission of Playscripts, Inc., which has published the entire text in an acting edition and which handles performance rights. Contact: Playscripts, Inc., Box 237060, New York, NY 10023, www.playscripts.com, 866-NEW-PLAY.

SCHOOLGIRL FIGURE. © 2004 by Wendy MacLeod. Reprinted by permission of Playscripts, Inc., which has published the entire text in an acting edition and which handles performance rights. Contact: Playscripts, Inc., Box 237060, New York, NY 10023, www.playscripts.com, 866-NEW-PLAY.

SEA OF TRANQUILITY. © 2004 by Howard Korder. Reprinted by permission of the Joyce Ketay Agency, 630 Ninth Ave. #706, New York, NY 10036. The entire text has been published in an acting edition by Dramatists Play Service, which handles performance rights. Contact: Dramatists Play Service, 440 Park Ave. S., New York, NY 10016, www.dramatists.com, 212-MU3-8960.

SECOND. © 2004 by Neal Utterback. Reprinted by permission of the author. The entire text has been published by New York Theatre Experience (www.newyorktheatreexperience.org) in *Plays and Playwrights 2005.*

SECURITY. © 2004 by Fountain Pen, Inc. Reprinted by permission of William Morris Agency, Inc., 1325 Ave. of the Americas, New York, NY 10019. The entire text has been published in an acting edition (in *Israel Horovitz: 5 Short Plays*) by Samuel French, Inc., which handles performance rights. Contact: Samuel French, Inc., 45 W. 25th St., New York, NY 10010, www.samuelfrench.com, 212-206-8990.

SEVEN RABBITS ON A POLE. © 2004 by John C. Picardi. Reprinted by permission of the author, c/o Fifi Oscard Agency, 110 W. 40th St., New York, NY 10018. The entire text has been published in an acting edition by Samuel French, Inc., which handles performance rights. Contact: Samuel French, Inc., 45 W. 25th St., New York, NY 10010, www.samuelfrench.com, 212-206-8990.